MW00463562

"The book you hold in yo
ral wisdom and insight. E
decades of ministry experience. You'll identify with Rich's challenges
and have the opportunity to see the Lord work in the life of a shepherd
of God's flock. The unique format will help both young men aspiring to
pastor and older men with decades of experience who want to learn how
to mentor younger pastors."

Brian Parks, Senior pastor, Covenant Hope Church, Dubai

"This is a book brilliantly conceived, creatively formatted, and superbly
executed. Phil Newton and Rich Shadden grabbed me at the beginning
and held me to the end. What struck me was the winsomeness of their
convincing humility throughout. A pastor with a half-century of experience and a protégé ten years into pastoral ministry have gifted us with
a treasure."

Ronnie Collier Stevens, Associate pastor, Harvest Church Memphis

"Dr. Newton's years of pastoral ministry experience are invaluable in
these wise exhortations and gracious encouragements to aspiring and
potential pastors, to those in their first pastorates, and to seasoned pastors as well. Even the format is pastoral. You will benefit in your own
ministry and in mentoring other pastors through their own peaks and
valleys."

Todd Wilson, Pastor, Grace Covenant Baptist Church, Vestavia
Hills, AL

"Every pastor needs a mentor. *Shepherding the Pastor* weds timely counsel, pastoral friendship, and practical wisdom, displaying both the how
and the why of mentoring. This book will encourage seasoned pastors to
be a mentor and new pastors to find one!"

Dave Kiehn, Senior Pastor, Park Baptist Church; regional coordi-
nator, Pillar Network; president, Institute of Theology and Mission

"If only I had read this book early in ministry! It took me many years,
many resources, and many mistakes to learn what *Shepherding the Pastor*
gathers in one enormously helpful volume. Please pull up a chair and
spend some time with Phil and Rich. They will shepherd you well."

David King, Senior pastor, Concord Baptist Church,
Chattanooga, TN; author of *Your Old Testament Sermon Needs
to Get Saved*

"Every pastor needs mentors. Some mentors are personal and present, daily speaking into the pastor's life. Other mentors instruct and encourage through published materials. Phil Newton and Rich Shadden have a proven track record of doing the former, and that's what makes *Shepherding the Pastor* so compelling. This is essential reading for every up-and-coming minister and helpful reading for ministers of all ages and tenures."

Jason K. Allen, President, Midwestern Baptist Theological Seminary and Spurgeon College

"This is a book I could not put down and is one I would love to place in the hands of every God-called pastor, elder, or overseer. It is a fountain of biblical and pastoral wisdom that will serve the body of Christ well for years to come."

Daniel L. Akin, President, Southeastern Baptist Theological Seminary

"Phil Newton has condensed into this excellent book a wealth of wisdom from the Bible and from his decades of pastoral experience. I love the unique format whereby Phil's pastoral protégé, Rich Shadden, presents his pastoral challenges and then explains how he applies Phil's counsel. The practical recommendations Phil makes at the end of each chapter are worth the price of the book. Every pastor in his early years of ministry would profit from reading this book."

Donald S. Whitney, Professor and Associate Dean, The Southern Baptist Theological Seminary; author of *Spiritual Disciplines for the Christian Life*

"I love Phil Newton, his pastor's heart, and his desire to mentor pastors. And I love that no matter what he's facing, he approaches it with the calm that comes from having walked with the Lord for a long time. In *Shepherding the Pastor*, we get to learn from Phil as he mentors Rich Shadden. I cannot commend this book highly enough. After decades of pastoral ministry, I'd happily sit at Phil's feet once again. I need it!"

Juan R. Sanchez, Senior pastor, High Pointe Baptist Church, Austin, TX

"First-time pastors need a lot of help! Where do you begin? How long should you stay? How do you navigate the rough waters of conflict and change? If you are looking for answers, read *Shepherding the Pastor*. This book offers practical help rooted in Scripture for the early years of the pastoral journey. It will help ministers of all ages. Buy two copies—one to read and one to share. Highly recommended!"

Ray Pritchard, President, Keep Believing Ministries

SHEPHERDING THE PASTOR

Help for the Early Years of Ministry

Phil A. Newton

&

Rich C. Shadden

New
Growth
Press

newgrowthpress.com

New Growth Press, Greensboro, NC 27401
newgrowthpress.com
Copyright © 2023 by Phil A. Newton and Rich C. Shadden

Cover Design: Studio Gearbox, studiogearbox.com
Interior Typesetting: Lisa Parnell, lparnellbookservices.com

ISBN: 978-1-64507-296-6 (Print)
ISBN: 978-1-64507-297-3 (eBook)

Library of Congress Cataloging-in-Publication Data on file

Printed in the United States of America

30 29 28 27 26 25 24 23   1 2 3 4 5

To my mom, Jane Taylor Newton,
who loves and prays for pastors,
especially this one.

To my wife, Kristy Jane Shadden,
my love, my helper, our journey.

Contents

Introduction

It's hard to be a pastor when you're not a Christian. Case in point: Berthold Haller, a young sixteenth-century pastor who was appointed as preacher for the Berne cathedral in Switzerland. Despite his exceptional gifts, Haller had not yet come to faith in Christ until he met Huldrych Zwingli, who mentored him as a father in the faith. After his conversion, Haller's ministry flourished. Finally, he preached about the Christ he knew from personal experience.

Yet not all welcomed young Haller's powerful preaching. As the trials of opposition grew, he wrote Zwingli, telling him of troubles in Berne and his desire to leave and take up the life of a scholar. Zwingli counseled patience and perseverance. "Don't abandon your post," he said. He wrote to his friend, "Such wild beasts need to be stroked gently and their growls tolerated for a space until, convinced by the constancy and depth of our perseverance, they are tamed by patience." Zwingli's letter put wind in Haller's sails. He wrote to Zwingli, "My soul has been awakened from its slumber, I must preach the gospel, Jesus Christ must be restored to this city, whence He has been so long exiled."[1] Haller needed Zwingli's mentoring to endure amid the strains of pastoral work.

Haller is not alone. Persevering as a pastor, particularly at one church, remains hard. Pastors need to establish healthy

1

patterns from the start so that when difficulties arise, they're prepared to keep serving Christ's church. Some of these patterns seem obvious: preaching faithfully, loving the flock, maintaining a strong marriage. Some things a pastor knows when he starts; other things he learns while at the wheel. To remain steady, to keep going as Haller did, we all need mentors. The purpose of this book is to provide some of that mentoring and to show how it might work in your ministry, whether you are a young pastor in need of a mentor or an older one who can also help shepherd others who pastor God's flock. We hope to give you a glimpse at how we've kept the mentoring relationship going as young pastor and mentor for over a dozen years. And we're continuing.

But let us offer a few caveats. This book is not about mentoring strategy. Nor is it about the history of mentoring. Nor does it provide a template for mentoring. Nor do we give a theological foundation for mentoring. All that can be found in a previous volume that Phil has written. Instead, we want you to get inside the skin of an ongoing mentoring relationship between a young pastor and a seasoned mentor. We want you to feel the young pastor's angst with challenges in ministry, while contemplating the value of an older pastor helping him navigate the pastorate. We want you to know something of our joy when we see the Lord work in difficult settings and when obstacles to maturity are overcome. We have a vision for young pastors becoming part of a church leadership team that uses God's Word to encourage, guide, and correct Christ's flock. Being a real church goes deeper than providing crowd-pleasing programs, and the pastoral issues we tackle will have a disciple-making vision of the church and its pastors in mind.

We will not provide answers to all your mentoring or pastoral questions. Instead, we want you to walk with us, listen in on our conversations, notice our emotions, see how we learn to rely on Christ, and learn with us how to move toward healthy pastor and church. We want to help readers value pastoral longevity and see a path toward that goal. To that end, we have in mind four foundational truths which weave their way throughout the ten chapters of this book. Without them, pastors won't last nor will they lead their congregations to be healthy.

Four essential components characterize pastoral longevity.

First, pastors must develop a deepening walk with Christ. A 2021 Lifeway survey of more than 1,500 pastors from various denominations showed that only half spent daily time alone with the Lord.[2] That's alarming! Only as pastors grow in the grace and knowledge of Christ, intensifying spiritual disciplines along the way, can they hope to faithfully and joyfully persevere. Christian character counts far more than gifts and abilities. We will interact in the book with conversations on this critical component.

Second, pastors must faithfully expound God's Word and declare "the whole counsel of God" (Acts 20:27). Their work needs to be Word-centered; they shouldn't dodge hard topics but let the Word by the Spirit do the work. We will put a lot of weight on the preaching component and how it worked into the mentoring process and Rich's ministry.

Third, pastors must continue learning from pastoral mentors. Martin Bucer mentored John Calvin. Calvin then mentored 120 pastors whom he sent to France over an eleven-year period. Even after they left, he counseled them through correspondence. When Andrew Fuller and William Carey began pastoral work in the eighteenth century, they regularly sought the counsel of Robert Hall Sr., who mentored these young pastors until his death. Alistair Begg learned pastoral ministry from Derek Prime during his time at Charlotte Chapel in Edinburgh. The two partnered in writing *On Being a Pastor*, giving evidence of Prime's ongoing influence as a mentor in Begg's pastoral ministry. When H. B. Charles Jr. began pastoral work, a mentor cautioned him to tap the brakes in making changes to his church's polity. His wise counsel kept Charles from faltering at the start.[3] We will attempt to model what this kind of ongoing mentoring looks like.

Fourth, pastors must grow in skillful, patient shepherding of the flock. Reading books on pastoral work gives some insights on how to shepherd a flock. But since every congregation is different, books can only do so much. So pastors need real experience with real people who are going through real problems or who have real complaints. Only real life hones a pastor's skills to disciple, counsel, comfort, encourage, and care for those under his charge. As he grows in shepherding, his joy in persevering through pastoral difficulties increases. Longevity is the fruit of such growth. That's what we're hoping you will discover as we tell our story.

We've written this book with these four lessons in mind. *Shepherding the Pastor: Help for the Early Years of Ministry* has a goal. We want to help pastors develop healthy patterns in ministry that will enable longevity. Further, we don't want them to pastor alone. We believe mentoring relationships that start before a man enters formal ministry should continue into the long stretch of pastoring. We hope to model healthy patterns and practices for mentors and mentees.

We approach the book from two perspectives. Phil has pastored for forty-four years, thirty-five of them at South Woods Baptist Church in Memphis, Tennessee. In 2021, Rich completed his tenth year of pastoring Audubon Park Baptist Church, also in Memphis. Phil started mentoring Rich before Rich began pastoring, and did not stop after Rich's installation. Phil has continued to journey with him as a mentor, helping Rich navigate the twists and turns of pastoring a local church.

A few years ago, Rich told Phil they should write a book. We both sensed that our story might encourage younger and older pastors to partner in pastoral ministry. To keep this mentor-mentee balance in mind, each chapter follows a pattern.

- First, Rich tells about a pastoral *challenge* he faced at Audubon Park.
- Second, Phil responds by offering *counsel* like he gave Rich and would give to other pastors in similar situations.
- Third, Rich follows with *application* for how the counsel worked into his rhythm of pastoral ministry.
- Fourth, Phil recommends *next steps* to help you know how to proceed when facing similar challenges.
- Finally, we identify some additional *resources* that might amplify the subject of the chapter.

We hope the journey in pastoral mentoring that we've written will serve fellow pastors for the first ten years and more, as we do the work of ministry together.

To help you know who is writing each section, this icon identifies Rich as the younger pastor being mentored.

 This icon identifies Phil as the more experienced pastor serving as a mentor.

Part 1
Sent Out

While they were worshiping the Lord and fasting,
the Holy Spirit said, "Set apart for me Barnabas and Saul for
the work to which I have called them."
Then after fasting and praying they laid their hands
on them and sent them off.

Acts 13:2–3

1.

Get Ongoing Training

 Young Pastor Rich Faces a Challenge

I sat and listened to a lecture in my pastoral ministry course on how to care for a church member suffering with an illness in the hospital. It sounded pretty cut-and-dried, merely theoretical. I wasn't a pastor at the time, but that day shortly arrived when I had to throw theory out the window. I stood at the bedside of a sick and dying member. While the lecture had some value, far more valuable were those times I walked with my pastoral mentor into a hospital room and watched as he cared for a sick member. No theory there, rather, I felt and sensed the way shepherds care for the flock in difficult times.

Consider medical training. Imagine you want to be a doctor. You apply to medical school, get accepted, and begin your studies. You learn everything you can possibly know about the human body and how to heal it. You know the textbooks front to back. All exams, aced. GPA, 4.0. You graduate with the highest honors. But throughout your entire experience, you never observe a surgery, you never meet with patients, and you never shadow doctors. You never listen to hearts beating and lungs inhaling, never stitch up a cut, never set a broken bone, never diagnose a disease, never comfort a patient. Then the day arrives when you become a practicing physician. How do you transfer book and classroom lectures into patient care? Your patients not only need your medical knowledge, but also your ability to care for them. Do you think you are prepared for longevity in your practice if you've not first walked with physicians who've endured the challenges of patient care? Do you think you might be a better physician if an experienced physician has mentored you?

Of course, medical doctors actually get this type of training. But it's often woefully absent for pastors. Here's how new pastors generally step into ministry, at least in America. A young man expresses a call to ministry. Then it's usually assumed he'll choose a seminary for training. He goes to seminary to learn theology, biblical languages, church history, and other important subjects. He even takes a class or two on "pastoral ministry." Upon his graduation, he looks for a job even though he has very little hands-on pastoral experience. He's never been mentored outside the classroom. No pastor has taken him under his wing to show him how to comfort the sick and dying. He's not learned how to navigate church conflict, or what the Bible teaches about a healthy church's polity. He made an A in his preaching class—he preached twice—but he's never done any sustained exposition under the watchful eyes of a mentor.

Typically, this is how a man gets trained for ministry. Certainly, his biblical knowledge has increased, but his pastoral skills remain underdeveloped. Before long, he'll learn that correct doctrine, as essential as it is, isn't enough for the long haul of pastoral ministry.

Church Confessions and Shepherding

For example, understanding the theological crisis that provoked the fourth century's Council of Nicea is important. It safeguards a biblical Christology: Jesus is the eternal Son of God and not merely a man, incarnate and not created. But shepherding a church member to navigate a relationship with a Jehovah's Witness—who denies the eternally divine nature of the Son—tests a completely different skillset. How do you help your church member distinguish a false sense of fellowship and instead pursue an evangelistic opportunity? That requires some pastoral skill.

Consider another example. Seminary teaches us that without sound doctrine a church veers toward disaster. In other words, it teaches us the value of a statement of faith. But how should a local church actually *use* its statement of faith? How should a new pastor evaluate a potential member's theology, using the statement of faith as his guide? Such a task requires more than classroom knowledge, and will be made easier with a mentor.

Mentoring gives an aspiring pastor the opportunity to observe how doctrine connects with practice. Obviously, pastors must be "able to teach" (1 Timothy 3:2). But shepherding Christ's blood-bought people is both didactic and relational. In other words, it mirrors the ministry of Jesus who not only taught sound theology but shepherded wounded, struggling, and helpless sheep: "When he saw the crowds, he had compassion for them, because they were harassed and helpless, like sheep without a shepherd" (Matthew 9:36).

Facing Reality

I thoroughly enjoyed seminary. I loved the give-and-take discussion, intense reading, and theologically rigorous assignments. But I really began to move from the theoretical to real-world application once I joined the pastoral internship at South Woods Baptist Church. The theology I was learning in seminary *and* at South Woods, coupled with practical ministry opportunities, trained me for the task ahead. The seminary taught theology in a lab; the local church brought theology into people's hurts, struggles, and spiritual needs.

Once I began pastoring, I realized I had much to learn (a decade later, that's still the case!). The internship gave me so much useful experience. I taught regularly. I preached a sermon series to the church. I observed counseling and, when appropriate, counseled others myself. I lent my hand to help on administrative projects. I visited the sick. I silently observed elders' meetings and membership interviews. I did all of this under the mentorship of the church's pastors, receiving encouragement and critical feedback along the way.

Mentoring allows future pastors to *make diagnoses, prescribe medication*, and *perform surgery* under the careful eye of experienced physicians. The patterns and practices I observed shaped my pastoral aspirations and formed a backbone for longevity. No matter a man's ministry setting—a church plant, a revitalization, or a church that's more-or-less healthy already—a man still needs training.

As I reflect on the last ten years of pastoring in a revitalization setting, I realize that without the mentoring before *and* throughout, my tenure might have been much shorter. I may have given up. Even more, I realize that a young pastor needs *ongoing mentoring* throughout the journey. One need only read the Pastoral Epistles to see how Paul urged Timothy and Titus to continue with steady hands.

Evaluating the Journey

You might be thinking, *How can I find a mentor? What if my church doesn't provide this opportunity? What if by going to seminary, I must relocate and find another church to train me? How can I continue to be mentored after I start pastoral ministry?* This chapter will begin to answer these important questions.

I've talked with Phil and other pastors since then about how best to approach pastoral training. There's no one-size-fits-all approach. But certain principles will serve you well as you seek out pastoral training in the local church. In the following pages, you'll learn from Phil about some of the training he sought out when formal mentoring had not yet caught on.

 Mentor Phil Offers Counsel

I came to faith in Christ as a fifteen-year-old. A year later, I sensed the Spirit's movement to preach the gospel. That was a strange desire for one who had a career in architecture in mind. But it wouldn't leave. I ate, slept, and drank preaching, even as a teenager. After some counsel from a couple of older friends, I announced this calling to a group of peers at an outdoor rally. My peers supported me, as did a few pastors from other churches in the area. My home pastor, however, offered no substantial encouragement or direction. He showed little interest in the newly converted teenagers, our passion to witness, and the movement toward ministry. He seemed to think that if I graduated from college and seminary, I'd figure it all out.

Really?

Pastoral ministry can be studied in an academic setting. I certainly tried that approach. But it's not always learned well in that setting, as Rich mentioned, any more than a physician learns everything in medical school. Not knowing any better, I did the best I could. In God's kindness, I had the opportunity as a college student to serve for a couple of years on a church staff. It was the pastor and me handling the work of ministry together. Whether he realized it or not, he mentored me. He gave me ample opportunities to test my ministry skills. I'm grateful for the time with him and that church. I learned to love pastoral ministry as I preached, taught, discipled, and shepherded the flock.

In my last year of seminary, I began pastoring a rural church almost three hours away. My wife, young daughter, and I spent each weekend living in a house the church owned while I preached twice on Sundays and made pastoral visits before returning to the seminary. Yet with my plunge into pastoring, I began to realize that Sunday came every week! Sermons would not prepare themselves. With a commitment to biblical exposition, I faced plenty of exegetical and homiletical struggles. I realized more and more that shallow wells won't sustain the pastor or congregation. If I would last, I had to grow in my spiritual disciplines, preaching preparation, and delivery. It didn't take long to realize that seminary classes alone couldn't sustain me. I needed the synthesis of seminary and mentoring, coupled with increased discipline, to keep up the pace of pastoral ministry even in this little church.

On graduation day, I moved "full-time" into this bi-vocational pastorate. And suddenly, I realized I could no longer see my professors during the week to discuss difficult challenges or unclear biblical texts. I felt alone. But so did another pastor a few miles down the road. We began a friendship as we experienced together the pitfalls and pinnacles of pastoral ministry. Every now and then, I would invite pastors to come in for a few days to preach. They were a balm to my soul, sources of wisdom in my multiple dilemmas. When I started as a pastor, I needed twenty years of wisdom to preach and shepherd. Of course, I didn't have it! But I did have friends, wise counselors who helped me press on.

Necessary Recognition

A diploma on the wall can blind us to our unpreparedness for ministry. We think we know our stuff. We made decent grades, and even got a few compliments on our sermons. We're ready to handle almost anything. Or so we think.

Sure, it's good to have confidence as we face the daily grind of ministry. But wrongly-placed confidence will likely result in some unhealthy patterns. We become unteachable, impatient, and unkind toward those we're supposed to serve. We claw away at trying to pastor when we're unsteady and unsure of *how to pastor*. We may think it's demeaning to admit inadequacies. But deep down, we know otherwise. Sometimes our flaws are glaring; other times, they lie beneath the surface. So how do we work through them?

Knowing a Few Essentials

I'm convinced that what we learn in our early years of pastoring does a lot to determine whether we'll endure. I've known countless pastors who started with enthusiasm, on fire for the Lord and the ministry he gave them to steward. And then, opposition comes. Or the enthusiastic pastor unexpectedly clashes with biblically unqualified leaders, or with longstanding power brokers who intend to put the new pastor under their thumb. Eventually, the pressure mounts and the pastor's tenure ends. Sometime the light flickers for a while; other times, it's seemingly snuffed out overnight. But the enthusiasm runs out, and so endurance ceases to be a viable option.

So, do you want to endure in ministry? Great. It's easy to say that—almost every pastor I've ever met says that. But if you want to actually *do it*, then you need to start preparing from the beginning. To that end, consider these five essential practices.

1. Maintain your walk with the Lord. One of the blessings of pastoral ministry is that it's our job to study and apply the Bible. And yet, one of the burdens of pastoral ministry is that it's *our job* to study and apply the Bible. In other words, it's easy to go through the motions. We prepare sermons, we pray at bedsides, we discuss the gospel with a new visitor. Outwardly, we may appear active and alive; inwardly, we may be dying or already dead.

To address this, we need to give attention to our souls. We need a regular devotional life, where we let God's Word bathe over us, where we meditate on it and pray through it, where we confess any sins the Holy Spirit reveals and comfort ourselves with the promises it assures. In doing so, we are steady and prepared for anything that comes our way—as 1 Timothy 4:7 says, trained for godliness. Without these patterns, we dry up. And when that happens, the enemy assaults us with vigor, trying to push us into sinful patterns that will wreck our lives and ministries. So, brother-pastor, take care of your soul.[1] Make sure, in the process of diligently caring for others, you haven't dangerously overlooked caring for yourself.

2. Shepherd like Jesus. Jesus models faithful shepherding as the one who "lays down his life for the sheep" (John 10:11). As you encounter Jesus in the Gospels, see how he cared for those around him. Notice how he showed tenderness to the downtrodden, spoke pointedly to the recalcitrant, and encouraged the fainthearted. Observe Jesus pursuing wandering sheep. Watch as Jesus washes his disciples' feet. Pause with wonder at Jesus laying down his life for the sheep.[2] He is our pastoral model.

3. Preach the Word with excellence. Give attention to preparing and preaching careful expositions from God's Word. Never allow preaching to become a secondary aspect. Preaching must be primary (see 2 Timothy 4:1–4). The pastor will need to discipline his life, arrange his schedule, and devote his energies to good hermeneutics, meditation, and homiletics. As he prayerfully prepares, his congregation's needs will be at the forefront of his mind. If he must let other things slide, so be it. But a pastor can't allow other demands to sidetrack him from faithful preaching.[3]

4. Grow in the grace of humble service. Pastors both old and young must regularly fight pride. It's a common adversary that has wrecked countless ministries. If you're a pastor, then you must always remember that you serve the sheep under the authority of the Chief Shepherd (see 1 Peter 5:1–5). Your members don't belong to you, but to the one who purchased them "with his own blood" (Acts 20:28). Pastors must set the example in Christian service even as they regularly call on their church to serve one another. Humble service battles against arrogance, ingratitude, and the sinful posture of authoritarianism.

Sadly, many churches are unhealthy because they've never enjoyed an extended ministry of faithfulness and fruitfulness. Similarly, many pastors have never enjoyed fruitfulness because they haven't stayed long enough to enjoy a congregation's love and trust. Put simply, more churches would be healthier if more pastors stayed longer. That doesn't mean the first church a pastor serves in will be where he spends his life. It could be, but that's unlikely. But it does mean pastors must learn to fight the temptation to climb the ladder of ministry to the neglect of the flock's long-term health. I suggest reading biographies of pastors who have exemplified endurance, such as those about John Calvin, John Bunyan, Charles Simeon, Charles Haddon Spurgeon, Jonathan Edwards, John Newton, John Sutcliff, Andrew Fuller, or Martyn Lloyd-Jones.

Fifty Years Later

I preached my first sermon in 1970. Seven and a half years later, I began my first pastorate. In the first nine years of pastoring, I served in three churches. The past thirty-five years, I've served one church: South Woods Baptist Church in Memphis. Over the years, a few practical matters stand out that will help to frame the discussion for longevity in ministry.

1. It's okay that I don't know it all. Pastoral ministry is full of situations where a decision has to be made but it's not obvious what to do. How do we navigate these very important yet very unclear moments? Of course, we start with God's Word. Our ministry and decision-making must be Scripture-centered. But in addition to that, we must be teachable. We must be willing to learn from others. Which reminds me . . .

2. Ask questions of fellow pastors, especially those with more experience. Much of what I've learned in ministry has come through asking questions, listening carefully, probing for clarity, and then filtering the responses into my context. So make sure you have older pastor friends. It's important to talk with peers your age, but it's best to learn from those who've been tested in the fire of ministry. Which reminds me again . . .

3. It's critical to have mentors. Mentoring relationships don't need to be overly formal. In fact, mentoring is really just one facet of an otherwise ordinary friendship. Over time, the hope is that deep friendships with like-minded brothers will spill over into your life to encourage you and shape your ministry. The Lord has given us examples of this in the Pastoral Epistles. Impoverished is the pastor who lacks trusted mentors. It there's no formal mentoring ministry to apply for, then take the step of asking one or two older pastors to occasionally meet for lunch to talk over pastoral life.

4. Keep a steady flow of good books before your eyes. Read regularly, broadly, deeply, and with appropriate application. When mentors were not available to me, I found mentors from the past who spoke into my life through their experience. Become friends with these fellow laborers. Their context will vary from yours, no doubt. But you can learn from their endurance and faithfulness. Don't rely on them in an absolute sense, but let them fill the gaps, deepen your pastoral insights, and come to your aid in the hard times. You'll find a few recommendations at the end of this chapter.

Reflecting on the past fifty years, I realize how the Lord seemed to put just the right person in my path when I needed to be sharpened or corrected, encouraged or admonished—when

I needed a good laugh or a good cry. I'm thankful for his sustaining grace.

 ## Young Pastor Rich Applies the Counsel

I want to mention two ways that the pastoral mentorship I received, especially from Phil, prepared me for my pastoral journey.

Comforting the Suffering Saints

Pastors are charged with comforting those who suffer, but how do we comfort the sick, the weak, and the dying? What should we do at the bedside of a man with terminal cancer? What do you say to an elderly lady whose health problems have mounted?

I remember riding with Phil to visit someone in the hospital. As we drove, he asked a question that had never crossed my mind: "What passage of Scripture do you think I should read?" That question shouldn't have shocked me, but it did. I had no idea what to say. I assumed we would listen, talk, and try to give encouragement. Of course, we would pray. But read Scripture? Wouldn't that be awkward?

About half an hour later, I sat in the patient's room. I watched as Phil opened his Bible to Psalm 46. Every word he read washed over this saint like a healing balm. I learned an important lesson that day about pastoral care. We aren't robots who calculate what Scripture passage to read in any given moment—*Here's the problem and here's the Scripture reference you need to hear.* Rather, we are mere people who need to pray for God's wisdom and mercy amid trials, people who need God's Word to strengthen their weary faith.

Sequential Exposition as the Main Diet

If a person eats a well-balanced diet, he will notice a difference in how he feels after an unhealthy meal. Indulging in a large pizza feels good for the moment, but a crash is coming. And if you eat a continuous flow of unhealthy meals, then the effects on one's health become obvious.

Preaching has similar effects on our spiritual health. If a congregation only hears topical preaching, then their maturity suffers. They become theologically lopsided and biblically anemic. Preaching aims, in part, to provide a well-balanced diet of God's Word. This seems best accomplished by preaching sequential expositional sermons through books of the Bible. How do we ensure we preach the whole counsel of God? We don't skip any of it. Thankfully, pastors modeled this pattern during my internship at South Woods, before I became a pastor of my own church, and gave the pastoral interns opportunities to practice.

On Sunday evenings, we preached through books of the Bible. I remember preaching through Colossians with my cohort. As we labored together, the congregation was fed as we received training under the guidance of the elders. In other words, our preaching practice happened *in the life of the church*, not in a laboratory. Not only did we encourage one another as aspiring pastors, but the congregation loved and exhorted us! The mutual edification was a beautiful sight to behold.

Find a Mentor

You may be the only pastor of the church you serve or will serve. But don't pastor in isolation. You need mentors, and the church you have the privilege of serving needs you to have mentors.

Mentor Phil Lists Some Next Steps

- Consider those whom the Lord has put into your life as mentors, whether formally or informally. How might you strengthen your mentoring relationships for the future? Do you need to discuss your spiritual disciplines and pastoral work with your mentors more frequently? If you don't have anyone mentoring you, spend the next few weeks praying for the Lord to raise up a mentor.

- What pastoral biography did you last read? How did it affect you? What did you learn and begin applying in your life? If it has been more than six months since you read a pastoral biography, secure one and start reading and learning from the past.

- In what areas do you find yourself impatient, frustrated, or despondent in pastoral ministry? Seek counsel from older pastors in how to handle these issues. Don't allow yourself to slump into sinful patterns in your walk and ministry. Deepen your time in the Word and in prayer. Confess your sins daily. Seek to walk in the Spirit. Add a good book on sanctification to your reading routine.

- Determine that you will bring pastoral mentors into your life as you serve Christ's church. Learn to be open with them about your struggles. Certainly, sift their counsel with the teaching found in God's Word.

Recommended Reading

Books about pastoring:

The Christian Ministry: With an Inquiry into the Causes of Its Inefficiency by Charles Bridges

Wise Counsel: John Newton's Letters to John Ryland Jr. edited by Grant Gordon

On Pastoring: A Short Guide to Living, Leading, and Ministering as a Pastor by H. B. Charles Jr.

40 Questions about Pastoral Ministry by Phil A. Newton

Books about the spiritual life:

Devoted to God: Blueprints for Sanctification by Sinclair B. Ferguson

An Infinite Journey: Growing toward Christlikeness by Andrew M. Davis

The Heart of a Servant Leader: Letters from Jack Miller by C. John Miller

Precious Remedies Against Satan's Devices by Thomas Brooks

Keeping the Heart: How to Maintain Your Love for God by John Flavel

The Bruised Reed by Richard Sibbes (which breathes the air of servant-heartedness, following Jesus's example, when caring for the flock)

Pastoral Biographies:

Here I Stand: A Life of Martin Luther by Roland H. Bainton

Andrew Fuller: Model Pastor-Theologian by Paul Brewster

Grace Abounding to the Chief of Sinners by John Bunyan

Spurgeon: A New Biography by Arnold A. Dallimore

Jonathan Edwards: A Life by George Marsden

The Life of Martyn Lloyd-Jones by Iain H. Murray

Charles Simeon: An Ordinary Pastor of Extraordinary Influence by Derek Prime

2.

Trust God's Sovereignty

 Young Pastor Rich Faces a Challenge

As a young boy, I remember taking trips with my family to the East Tennessee mountains. To get to wherever we were staying, we often drove on winding roads made up of loose gravel. I'm certain we were safe (I think), but I admit the thought of plunging down the side of a mountain never fully left my mind. Those trips mixed incredible beauty with overwhelming uncertainty.

Pastoral ministry isn't all that different. It's like a trip through the mountains with sudden ups and down, marked by abrupt stops followed by bursts of momentum. The twists and turns are marked by pain and joy, sorrow and gladness, gut-wrenching frustration and boisterous laughter. Some may wonder, *Why would you even want to do this?* As I think about that question, I recall the twists and turns of my own journey toward pastoral ministry.

I first think of First Baptist Church in Martin, Tennessee. That's where my love for Christ and his church began. The saints there taught me the gospel. They discipled me. That's where I first felt a desire to shepherd God's flock, and over time the church affirmed this desire. So ultimately, I went to seminary.

While in seminary, my wife and I joined South Woods Baptist Church. We flourished there as we heard the Word and enjoyed gospel-centered community. I distinctly remember visiting South Woods one Sunday evening as the church addressed a painful situation. Heaviness filled the room. I could sense the sadness of the people—and yet, I was strangely encouraged. Why? I had read about church discipline in Matthew 18 and 1 Corinthians 5, and briefly discussed it in my systematic theology course. But I'd never *seen* it. I was blown away. As an aside: if you're looking for a healthy church, look for a church that practices obedience in the hard things like church discipline.

We quickly joined South Woods. For two and a half years, we immersed ourselves in the life of the church. With increasing clarity, we saw what a local church ought to look like. We learned how to pursue obedience with joyful seriousness. Our church wasn't perfect, but we sought to honor Christ and obey the Scriptures in everything. I took every opportunity I could to learn and grow, especially from the elders.

I eventually took part in the pastoral mentorship I've already described. And finally, for about the last year and a half, the Lord began to prepare us mentally and emotionally to leave. Why would we leave such an edifying place? Well, through the church, the Lord had opened my eyes to the need for church revitalization. The thought of being used by God to lead a dying church toward health invigorated my soul. So my wife and I began praying for an opportunity. For a year and a half, we prayed.

Eventually, Audubon Park Baptist Church in Memphis showed interest in me. Almost immediately, questions popped up. *How do I handle the interview process? Are there certain questions I need to prepare for? How do I handle difficult or misunderstood theological questions (Calvinism was a controversial topic during this time)? Do I lay all my theological cards on the table? What questions do I need to ask them?*

I needed help, so I talked with Phil. Here's what he told me: "Trust God's sovereignty and speak truthfully, but with discernment." This counsel unwound a coil of anxiety by reminding me that God is sovereign and in control.

Mentor Phil Offers Counsel

Jesus Christ cares for the church. He laid down his life in an atoning death for the church. He modeled love, humility, and service for the church. He trained an unlikely group of men to carry on his work of establishing and discipling the church. He even invested them with his authority to speak the eternal, authoritative word upon which he would build his church. Amazingly, Jesus even sent letters to local congregations at the beginning of Revelation. He cares for the church.

Jesus means to equip and build up the church unto unity, maturity, and service through the gift of qualified pastor-teachers (see Ephesians 4:11–16). A healthy church will raise up and then send out such men. Put simply, a church shouldn't only think of itself. If we look at the book of Acts, we see how the church moves forward and expands to reach people from "every tribe and language and people and nation" (Revelation 5:9). Every local church should follow this example, which means every local church should seek to "send out laborers into his harvest" (Matthew 9:38).

Healthy Incubators

Some churches take this responsibility to heart. Others don't think about it. A man who aspires to pastoral work will not find much help in the latter. Sadly, I was in such a church as a teenage "preacher boy." While the pastor and church at large gave little to no thought of training aspiring preachers, a few in the church did. They were sharp tools in God's workshop to whittle away at my lack of discipline, bad theology, and flawed understanding of the gospel and the church. They laid the groundwork upon which others built. It's not that my preparation toward pastoral work was on a rocket-launch trajectory. It was more like Rich's description of the mountain with gravel roads. As I read his words I thought, *That was my early life preparing for ministry.* But thank God, Christ cares for his churches. By his multiplied mercies, he brought different people into my life to hone and shape me. These churches chipped away at rough spots, gave me opportunities to minister, and cheered me on.

As I prepared for ministry, I desperately needed a healthy church. I needed pastors who would put me under their wings and into their ministry workshop until I was ready. Instead, I learned a lot of things the hard way—and I mean *a lot of things!* My experience has affected how I've sought to lead my congregation in training those the Lord brings our way, which reminds me of Rich.

Fairly quickly, our elders noticed Rich's giftedness and pastoral heart. Furthermore, we knew he would face some difficulties candidating for and beginning to serve in a church in need of revitalization. Such works require careful, yet firm labors. Generally speaking, churches in need of revitalization don't realize the extent of their need. Their worship has become rote. Their passion for discipling has faded, replaced by slaps on the back and superficial relationships. Their witness is dim, stripped of the attractive beauty of the gospel.

Who wants to pastor a church like that? Someone like Rich! Someone who wants to be used by God to shepherd his saints back to life. Christ cares for his church, so he loads some aspiring shepherds with a desire to see what a church might become when the gospel returns to its center.

Candidating for a Church

Let's think about candidating for a church like that. What do you say? What do you *not* say? How do you make the most of your time with the pastoral search committee (or whatever it's called)? In some ways, these interviews can be like trying to ask a nuclear scientist questions about his work. You surely don't know enough about his profession to even ask the right questions. It's often like that with the godly and well-intentioned folks who make up pastoral search committees. They don't know enough about the church and pastoral ministry to ask the right questions. So what does wisdom look like in these situations? How will a candidate respond? First of all, he won't unload a textbook full of technical answers. He'll try to bring his questioners along, gently clarifying mistaken perspectives and trying to give a clearer picture of pastoral work.

One candidating experience of my own (years before I started mentoring other pastors) stands out. My wife and I met with the pastoral search committee, and they began to ask me a few questions. They asked what I liked about ministry, what I thought about the church, what I considered my strengths and weaknesses, and things like that. The only theological question they asked was a predictable one: "How does someone get saved?"

Then one fellow who had been quiet decided he would speak up. This was in the early 1980s. The charismatic movement had swept through many evangelical churches and impacted communities. Churches in their area had split over charismatic teaching. This fellow knew he had heard something about it, and all he knew was that it was *bad*. So he asked me, "What do you think about that *crismatic* movement?" I said, "Do you mean the charismatic movement?" "Yeh," he responded, "that's what I mean."

Immediately, I knew he understood nothing about the charismatic movement, its beginnings, its positive characteristics, its problematic areas, or what churches like his might learn from it. I could just as well have started telling him what I knew about nuclear science! But in a moment of restraint, I began to trace the movement, some of its adherents, how it had affected churches in good ways and some of the downsides, some of its errors, and how it had revived a much-needed discussion of the work of the Holy Spirit, although it needed theological clarity. After what I momentarily considered a brilliant explanation, I realized it fell on deaf ears. He didn't have the theological categories or biblical foundation to understand anything I said. Nor could I effectively communicate with him apart from bridging this knowledge gap. In other words, I failed.

Prospective pastors need to be wise when they sit down with a search committee. It's possible your committee may have razor-sharp theology. But it's unlikely, especially if you're entering into a revitalization work. Generally speaking, these folks have low expectations. They just want someone to come for a few years before moving on to the next stop. They're desperate because they assume no one wants to plant roots down with them and shepherd them to health. And so, with no ill intentions, they ask perfunctory questions.

I told Rich that he would probably get asked if he was a Calvinist, since at the time of his candidating lots of talk circulated about it. I knew at least one committee member had told some people in our church not to have anything to do with Calvinists: *They're bad. They wreck churches. They don't believe in evangelism.* So how would Rich answer that question and similar ones?

1. Always define what is being asked. If it happens to be Calvinism, then ask a follow-up question: "What do you mean by *Calvinist?* There's lots of disagreement on that question." If you're candidating at a Baptist church that is spooked by the idea of a Calvinist's supposed hatred of evangelism, then you may even want to remind them that many Baptist forefathers, including William Carey and Charles Spurgeon, called themselves Calvinists. They were exemplary churchmen *and* exemplary evangelists. Assuming you respond with graceful tact, you will likely defuse the conversation.

2. Answer with Scripture. If you can't defend what you believe from God's Word, then the committee would be right to reject you. But if you're able to appeal to Scripture for support, then you're more likely to satisfy the questioner. In fact, they may even discover they actually agree with you!

3. Avoid using theological buzzwords. You can use certain words around seminary classmates and fellow pastors. But remember: theological terms and common cultural phrases almost always need to be defined with clearly-stated biblical categories and concepts. If your conversation calls for using theological terms, then explain them in a simple way as part of your response. Your goal should be to speak the truth of God's Word in love and with patience (Ephesians 4:15–16; 2 Timothy 2:24–25). With a gentle spirit, explain any difficult terms.

4. Don't hide who you are. In other words, don't let misunderstandings or vagueness persist, even if they may help you get the job. Make sure those on the committee know where you stand, even if where you stand is in fact in opposition to their current understanding or practice. If they're already in agreement with you, great! They'll appreciate your biblical clarity. If they're not, then the questioner might just realize they have far more interest in someone like you than they originally imagined.

5. Trust in the sovereignty of God. You don't want to begin a pastorate under pretense. Time with a pastor search committee is only the start. In fact, much of what a committee asks they forget (at least, that's my experience). You've given them clear answers which they approved of at the time. But six months later, some will have memory lapses about your theology, your philosophy of ministry, and your expectations and hopes for the church. That may happen. If it does, trust the Lord. He put you there, not to be comfortable or without conflict. He put you there to shepherd this struggling flock to health, unity, and maturity. You need not toss in your bed at night wondering why you accepted their call. The Lord of the church put you there. And he, through much grace and patience with you, will keep you there to care for his people.

Along the way, he will be shaping you to shepherd more like Jesus.

Jesus cares for his church enough to give churches faithful men. Pastoral search committees should ask lots of good, hard questions about theology, ecclesiology, and methodology. When they don't know enough to know what to ask, then the gracious candidate should tell them anyway—not as a know-it-all, but as a shepherd who wants to care for God's people with patience and grace.

 Young Pastor Rich Applies the Counsel

I remember walking into the church office where the search committee arranged to meet me. I felt mixed emotions. But Phil's counsel kept rattling around in my brain. I remember thinking, *God, you are sovereign. Your purposes will be accomplished. So help me be loving, clear, transparent, and trust you whatever the outcome.* Then we began our conversation.

The committee was kind. They kept asking about various outworkings of my theology rather than my theology itself. For example, they asked about style of music. They didn't ask me to articulate my understanding of biblical worship; they simply wanted to know if I preferred the Gaithers or the Gettys. They asked me how I would handle conflict, but not about my understanding of what the Bible teaches on reconciliation. Because I was young and inexperienced, they wondered if I could resolve conflicts among both staff and members.

I sympathized with these questions. A dying church is dying for a reason. *Nothing has worked.* That's the mindset. So they just wanted to know if I had answers that *would work.*

But I knew the Holy Spirit through God's Word must do the work. In my power, I can produce zero kingdom results. So throughout the conversation, I simply tried to point to how God's Word could be applied to the life of their church.

Near the end of our time, an elderly lady—who remains a Christ-loving, faithful servant of the church today—asked a pointed theological question: "What do you believe about Calvinism?" I knew what to do. I asked her, "Well, what do you mean by that?" Her question then became more precise. "What do you believe about predestination?" I took Phil's advice, turned to Ephesians 1, and walked through my understanding of predestination. I had no idea how the committee would respond. But once they heard that I believe we must preach the gospel to all, that settled it for them.

Mentor Phil Lists Some Next Steps

- If you will soon be meeting with a pastoral search committee, resolve not to be on the defensive. Be yourself. Most importantly, handle questions as a shepherd.
- Prepare. Think through how you might respond to various questions. You don't need to be an expert on all issues. Rather, demonstrate how to move from the issue *du jour* to the centrality of the gospel.
- Commit your interview to the Lord. Trust his wise providence. Should a church invite you to consider a call to pastor them, be careful not to swell with pride over your performance with the search committee. The sovereign Lord has opened the door for you to be considered. He alone can work out the details. Trust him with humility.

Recommended Reading

Phil offers his perspective on how churches should train potential pastors and missionaries in his book *The Mentoring Church*. Also be sure to check out his book *40 Questions about Pastoral Ministry*.

One of the best stories about revitalization is Andy Davis's article, "The Reform of First Baptist Church of Durham," about his experience as a pastor in Durham, North Carolina. It is available online at the 9Marks website.[1] You also might read the following:

Facing Snarls and Scowls: Preaching through Hostility, Apathy, and Adversity in Church Revitalization by Brian Croft and James B. Carroll (for a helpful pastoral look at revitalization)

Nine Marks of a Healthy Church by Mark Dever

The Shepherd Leader: Achieving Effective Shepherding in Your Church by Timothy Z. Witmer

Any of the books in the 9Marks Building Healthy Churches collection

Part 2
The Beginning Years

As I urged you when I was going to Macedonia,
remain at Ephesus so that you may charge certain persons
not to teach any different doctrine.

1 Timothy 1:3

3.

Now What? Preach the Word

 Young Pastor Rich Faces a Challenge

I stared at the wall while my body sank into paralysis. Sitting in my office less than a month after the church voted to affirm me as their pastor, Phil's words ran through my mind. I can still hear them clearly: "After two to three months you'll ask, *What have I gotten myself into?*"

He was right. A few weeks in, I was already asking that question!

The work of a pastor never ends. There's always a sermon to prepare, a member to shepherd, administrative responsibilities to accomplish, a marriage to counsel, a funeral to conduct, a leader to disciple, and the list goes on and on. I quickly learned as a young pastor how unorganized and unfocused I was. I felt like a deer gazing into the headlights of an oncoming car, and there was no time to jump out of the way!

The church welcomed our family well. Quite frankly, I'm not sure how they could have welcomed us any better. My wife, Kristy, and I knew we were exactly where God wanted us. We immersed ourselves into the congregation. I had what I thought was a great plan to build relationships with the members. I intended to visit their homes, sit in their classes on Sunday mornings, and take all the opportunities I could to be with them. I wanted to spend the first six months to a year getting to know the members of Audubon Park on a more personal level.

To put it simply, I overshot. Before I knew it, I was juggling too many administrative responsibilities. I led a staff of ten people who were hired to serve a congregation of eighty members. Four of the staff were full-time. Before this, the only prior experience I had leading anyone was my family and a group of young college men I discipled—all it took for them to show up was pizza and the Bible! You can imagine how intimidated I felt.

I understood the importance of preaching, disciple-making, soul care, prayer, and other biblical responsibilities for the pastor. But when the lights came on and I was on the field, the jolt of the moment dizzied me. I had no idea how I would be able to do all that people were expecting me to do. The expectations seemed too great.

Funerals and Sundays

During my first three years at Audubon Park, I preached more than forty funerals. To be honest, I didn't have any idea what to do. And in almost every case, I didn't know the member because I was new. During those weeks, my administrative responsibilities flew out the door as I focused on visiting with the family to learn more about their loved one. I didn't want to mess up. Before I knew it, Saturday arrived, and I was conducting a funeral service.

God was so gracious in that period. I remember walking down the center aisle to the front of the funeral chapel and seeing some of the elderly widows in our congregation sitting together. One of them got my attention and said, "We're cheering for you!" That still fills me with joy. Those godly ladies wanted to encourage their new pastor.

I did my best to lead the service, preach a biblically faithful funeral sermon, and comfort the family. After the service, we arrived at the graveside. I remember asking the funeral director, with a confused look on my face, "Where do I stand?" He helped me. "Stand at the head of the casket," he said. I closed our time together at the graveside and breathed a sigh of relief. I had done my best. And yet, a daunting reality hung over my head: Sunday was coming. In fact, it was the next day! I had so much sermon preparation left to do. I hadn't prioritized my week, and so Saturday night would be a long one.

If you've been pastoring for any length of time, I'm sure the previous paragraphs sound familiar to you. Perhaps they caused a chill to run down your spine. It's a hard-won lesson for every pastor: he needs to be careful and intentional with his schedule. Most likely, no one will show up on your first day and tell you what to do and when to do it. So you must learn early on how to prioritize what Scripture prioritizes. All your responsibilities are important. But how do you prioritize? After that, how do you organize and actually accomplish your priorities?

As I sat there staring at the wall, I knew what to do. I picked up the phone and called Phil. I explained what I was going through, and his counsel was both helpful and biblically faithful. While many responsibilities loom before you, one stands above all the others like a California redwood. Prioritize all other pastoral responsibilities around this one exhortation: Preach the Word!

Mentor Phil Offers Counsel

My dad was our small town's funeral director. He knew a lot of pastors, so I had plenty of opportunities as a teenager, newly desirous to preach, to fill area pulpits. I'm not suggesting that my preaching was any good. In fact, I'm thankful that my memory has failed to store many specifics. But all these years later, one thing stands out: I needed to preach God's Word to these people.

Preachers of God's Word must be students of God's Word. We must so immerse ourselves in the biblical text that we have something to say to our people. Of course, this doesn't happen quickly. Even a seminary degree can't guarantee that a freshly minted pastor will exposit the Scriptures with clarity and winsomeness. But he must try. By all means, he must set the preaching of God's Word as the most important aspect of his ministry.

After Jesus engaged in a particularly grueling day of ministry, early the next morning he rose before the sun peaked across the horizon and sought a quiet place to pray. The disciples looked for him. When they finally found him, they urged Jesus to return to local action. "Everyone is looking for you," they told him. In other words, *we have things planned for you: people to see, sick to heal, demons to cast out. Everyone wants a piece of you, and we're doing our best to accommodate them. Come on! Let's go.* But Jesus shocked them by following his own agenda: "Let us go on to the next towns, that I may preach there also, for that is why I came out" (Mark 1:38). Jesus lived with the priority of preaching the good news.

Similarly, shortly before the apostle Paul's death, he told Timothy, "I charge you in the presence of God and of Christ Jesus, who is to judge the living and the dead, and by his appearing and his kingdom: preach the word; be ready in season and out of season; reprove, rebuke, and exhort, with complete patience and teaching" (2 Timothy 4:1–2). The seriousness of the exhortation couldn't be stronger. *Preach the Word.*

Gravity in Preaching

Unless a pastor understands the priority of preaching, lesser things will take over his ministry. The tyranny of the urgent will sidetrack his goal to spend devoted time exegeting and mining the biblical text. It will distract him from praying over his text. It will encourage him to rush through application to his people. Does the pastor need to counsel, visit, disciple, train, and organize? Certainly. That's part of his work and the work of the church. But he must first preach God's Word.

At one point in my ministry, I preached through Acts 6 and came under conviction that my priorities were out of balance. Luke writes, "It is not right that we should give up preaching the word of God to serve tables. . . . But we will devote ourselves to prayer and to the ministry of the word" (vv. 2, 4). I confessed to the congregation that the Spirit had deeply convicted me, so I was reordering my weekly schedule to spend mornings in the study preparing to preach. I assumed the congregation would understand, so let's just say I *was not* ready for the backlash that came my way. The church wasn't familiar with biblical preaching; they hadn't had a pastor who studied and prepared. So they reacted strongly *against* the idea. They thought I wanted to hide in my study so that I could stay away from them! That's what they heard.

The murmuring became so severe that I had to address the matter again the following Sunday. Here's what I decided to do. They may not want the Word but by God's grace, I'm going to work hard to give it to them anyway. They may prefer the pastor to neglect the study for more mundane things, but I refuse, as one who must stand before God to give an account of how I discharged my pastoral responsibilities (Hebrews 13:17). Was it a challenge? Yes, every week. Did I sometimes succumb to devoting my time to lesser matters instead of the Word? Yes, it happened. Yet some of the patterns that slowly worked into my weekly rhythm in preparation for Sundays got established in that crucible. By his grace, the Lord made my preaching and my preparation fruitful. Perhaps even more importantly at that stage in ministry, the Word was starting to work deeply in my own life.

A Mouthpiece for the Text

Churches need the regular preaching of God's Word. But guess what? Preachers need it too. A preacher needs to wrestle with the text, to see himself in light of God's revelation, and to cling to the gospel as he repents of sins revealed and worships the Lord who gave himself for his people. Week after week, his job remains more or less the same: agonize over properly interpreting the Word, pray for his flock, and then in weakness and humility stand before the congregation as, in the words of J. I. Packer, a mouthpiece for the text.[1] A pastor will not grow except by faithfulness in the study that spills over in the pulpit. A pastor may be popular and even successful in the eyes of the world without this kind of diligence, but he will not have a word necessary for his flock as they walk through trials, struggle with loss, and mourn over their sins. A pastor's sermon preparation sharpens his pastoral skills.

It's not an overstatement to say that his pulpit ministry strengthens every aspect of his pastoral work. But faithful preaching doesn't happen by accident. It can't wait until Friday or Saturday, and it requires more than scouring a few commentaries to cobble together a semblance of a Sunday sermon. I've faced that struggle. Procrastination often proved a scourge to me in younger days, as I failed to measure my week, pace my study, and remember that Sunday came every first day of the week. Over time, I realized I had to be ready to make Christ known. I grew tired of poor preparation, which finally broke me of the bad habits that left the church starved and me anxious.

I'm writing this chapter fifty-one years to the day since I publicly announced my aspiration for ministry. I've learned a few things about preaching in half a century. Perhaps most importantly, as I told Rich early on in his ministry, you just have to let other things go. Someone else can do certain tasks, but no one else is going to stand in your place on Sunday to open the Word. Your administrative skills will not change and revitalize your congregation. Neither will your single-handedly taking on every counseling case. But patient, faithful preaching will. You don't need a double major or triple major. Major on preaching the Word. God has promised to bless his Word proclaimed and taught to the church. "Him we proclaim, warning everyone and teaching everyone with all wisdom, that we may present everyone mature in Christ" (Colossians 1:28). Through the Holy Spirit's power, let the Word do the work of uprooting sin, convicting of unbelief, producing repentance, imparting faith, and following Christ. This isn't a call to hide in your office and "study" fifty hours a week. But it is a call to protect a sufficient slice of your schedule so that study and preparation never slips out of your hands due to seemingly more urgent and important issues.

Young Pastor Rich Applies the Counsel

When I moved on from my internship and began my ministry at Audubon Park, I knew preaching was important. Both Scripture and my own mentors had taught me that the Lord uses the preaching of his Word to transform individuals and churches. By the grace of God we plant and water, but it is God alone "who gives the growth" (1 Corinthians 3:7). And yet, when I actually became a pastor I realized how this most important task can easily get pushed aside.

Thankfully, when I arrived at Audubon Park, that church expected preaching. But the kind of preaching they received from me was not quite what they anticipated. After one Sunday, I walked to my car and noticed a piece of paper taped to my window. As I drew closer, I realized it was a clip from a newspaper cartoon. The gist of the joke was simple: I needed to add more humor to my preaching. While I had no qualms about appropriate humor in preaching (see: Charles Spurgeon), I don't think it should be forced. Besides, there are naturally-funny people and naturally-good storytellers. Those traits can be used to help expound God's Word. But if they consistently overshadow the exposition of the text, then one has failed as a preacher.

A church shouldn't walk away from a sermon struck by a preacher's charisma or creativity. They should be struck by

Scripture and how the Holy Spirit is already applying it to their lives. The goal of preaching, as Mark Dever puts it, is to "make the main point of the text the main point of the sermon."[2] In other words, expositional preaching aims to herald what God has already said in his Word. It's not a license to be boring or to offer a running commentary, but to faithfully expose and apply God's Word from your mouth with your personality to the minds and hearts of those who are listening. With both God's help and the longsuffering of a *patient* congregation, I've made this my practice for the last ten years.

Initially, I preached through Philippians for nine months. During that time, God used his Word to reveal the disunity in our congregation. There were saints who loved being taught the Word and wanted to see the church grow in gospel unity. But there were also those who wanted unity built around things other than what Scripture prioritizes. That became plain. Little did I know, a storm was brewing.

After working through Philippians, I began a two-year journey through the gospel of John. God used two themes in that book—his sovereignty and Jesus's interactions with the Pharisees—to uproot idols and set the church on a healthy trajectory. Nevertheless, by the time I finished the gospel of John, the church was a mess. But God was in control. And now, looking back, I see his sovereign hand at work as he uprooted sin and gave us a deeper hunger for the Scripture. The same Word that repelled many nourished others. And over time, those who wanted God's Word increased. What I didn't quite see during the storm was the galvanizing of God's people. Division erupted. Factions formed. Efforts to have me fired arose. And I was afraid. But God honored his Word. And I didn't get fired—at least not yet!

I learned a lot during these turbulent years. Perhaps what stands out most is this: pastors must feed the flock entrusted to their care, no matter the outcome. There were certainly moments when I believed my final day at Audubon Park had come. It's possible that you may follow this counsel and get fired as a result. But that's okay. After all, who are you seeking to please? Paul posed the same question as he sought to teach the Galatian churches the true gospel: "Am I now seeking the approval of man, or of God?" (Galatians 1:10). Charles Spurgeon explained the call to keep preaching Christ this way:

> Suppose a number of persons were to take it into their heads that they had to defend a lion, full-grown king of beasts! There he is in the cage, and here come all the soldiers of the army to fight for him. Well, I should suggest to them, if they would not object, and feel that it was humbling to them, that they should kindly stand back, and open the door, and let the lion out! I believe that would be the best way of defending him, for he would take care of himself; and the best "apology" for the gospel is to let the gospel out.[3]

Fellow pastor, keep letting the lion out of the cage.

 Mentor Phil Lists Some Next Steps

- Read a classic book on preaching, such as *Preaching and Preachers* by Martyn Lloyd-Jones, *The Art of Prophesying* by William Perkins, *Between Two Worlds* by John Stott, *Preaching Christ in All of Scripture* by Edmund Clowney, or *The Supremacy of God in Preaching* by John Piper. Use this book to evaluate your present plan for preparation and preaching. Record any changes you commit to make in your preaching ministry. You could ask a pastor friend to read the book along with you so that you might have discussions about its implications.

- Develop a preaching plan for the next three to six months. Prayerfully decide what book(s) of the Bible you will preach. Identify the breakdowns of the texts. Organize your study schedule to excel in preparation. Get into a rhythm of planning your preaching three to twelve months in advance.
- Read or listen to faithful biblical expositions on the portion of God's Word you are preparing to preach. Learn from other preachers. Note their reverence for the Word. Identify their explanation and application. As you do this, avoid the folly of comparing yourself to another preacher, and don't copycat. Simply learn from them. Let your soul be fed. Consider that the Lord has called you to shepherd a particular flock with the unique personality and gifts he has entrusted to you. Prepare well and preach with fresh awareness of the ministry given to you.

Recommended Reading

In addition to the books on preaching noted above, consider *Expositional Preaching: How We Speak God's Word Today* by David Helm in the 9Marks Building Healthy Churches series.

For more on planning your preaching schedule, see pages 191–206 of Phil's book, *40 Questions about Pastoral Ministry*.

4.
Aim for Longevity and Biblical Reform

 Young Pastor Rich Faces a Challenge

In their book *The Trellis and the Vine*, which is essential reading
for pastors, Colin Marshall and Tony Payne use a helpful illus-
tration in describing local church ministry:

> Churches are a mixture of trellis and vine. . . . Just as
> some sort of framework is needed to help a vine grow,
> so Christian ministries also need some structure and
> support. It may not be much, but at the very least
> we need somewhere to meet, some Bibles to read
> from, and some basic structures of leadership within
> our group. All Christian churches, fellowships, or
> ministries have some kind of trellis that gives shape
> and support to the work. As the ministry grows, the
> trellis also needs attention. Management, finances,
> infrastructure, organization, governance—these all
> become more important and more complex as the
> vine grows.[1]

As pastors train the saints for the work of ministry,
they must give attention to both trellis work and vine work.

Structure (trellis work) is important for the reasons noted above. But pastors are primarily responsible to ensure that vine work—such as teaching the Word of God, pastoral counseling, discipleship among the body, and evangelism—takes place. Put simply, vine work should receive more attention than trellis maintenance. But good trellises will support and enable the vines to grow.

Too often, pastors and churches become more concerned with trellises and, in the process, neglect the vine work. No doubt, the growth of a church may require giving more attention to trellis work. For example, they may need to hire additional staff or create some organizing mechanism for small groups or Sunday school classes. But structure also needs to be examined when churches are in *decline*. Marshall and Payne go on to say, "Perhaps trellis work has taken over from vine work. There are committees, structures, programs, activities, and fundraising efforts, and many people put lots of time into keeping them all going, but the actual work of growing the vine falls to a very few."[2] As too many trellises grow, the vine gets choked out.

When I arrived at Audubon Park, I found a lot of trellises. The church had begun in 1944. A group of Christians saw a need for a church to be planted in the neighborhood where we still meet. Praise God! Over decades, Audubon Park experienced extraordinary growth. At its numerical peak, membership reached over a thousand. As membership grew, so did the number of trellises. Ministries, staff positions, programs, committees, and events boomed. But for various reasons, the church declined. When I arrived in 2011, eighty members voted to call me as senior pastor. I hadn't yet fully grasped that the church, though small, spent much of its energy on its large number of trellises. Naturally, the vine withered.

Too Many Trellises

We essentially had three categories of trellises. First, we had staff and lay leadership, which primarily consisted of paid pastoral staff, support staff, and the deacon body that oversaw all the various trellises. Second, we had committees made up primarily of church members who carried out various ministry tasks. Third, we had a Sunday school trellis that functioned as the educational tool of the church. There was also a fourth category that wasn't technically a part of the trellis—but oh my, did it operate with reckless abandon! This fourth category was an unofficial but influential group of longstanding church members.

The staff operated as if the church had hundreds of members, not eighty. We had four full-time employees, including me. In case it's not obvious, a congregation of eighty members, mostly retired, meeting in a facility built to accommodate more than a thousand with significant operating costs, will have extreme difficulty supporting four full-time employees, even without the other part-time staff (which we had too!).

I remember one Christmas in those early years when a member of the congregation decided the staff needed a Christmas bonus. This had been the generous practice of the church in previous years when they had ten times the attendance. However, the church was already unable to support the staff we had without losing significant money each month. Out of sheer generosity, this man gave a monetary Christmas bonus to each staff member. I appreciated his generosity, but I couldn't help but notice a flashing warning light. If a church cannot support its existing staff, then the staff is no longer ministering to the church but suffocating it financially. It was hard to admit, but the staff needed to downsize so the church could focus on vine work.

I also discovered that our deacon body of eight men functioned as a hybrid-elder board who made many important decisions but rarely taught or shepherded. They had to approve any recommendations before they were taken to the church. While these men were godly servants, their diaconate role was misunderstood because the church hadn't yet learned the difference between that office and the office of elder.

Beyond that, I remember counting fifteen committees in those early years. We had committees for baptisms, deacon selection, decorations, finances, personnel, flower arrangements, building and grounds, telephone announcements, audio and visual aids, insurance, Sunday school, and more! We even had a committee on committees to oversee all the committees! The difficulty of maintaining all these committees became obvious: there weren't enough people to serve on them. Rather than downsizing the trellises so that more emphasis could focus on vine work, we spent an inordinate amount of time, money, and attention to keep our already-dead trellises from collapsing.

For example, our church's Sunday school framework consisted of nursery classes, children's classes, a youth department, and an age-graded class structure for young adults through seniors. The Sunday school committee's main task was to annually nominate teachers for each class. Again, the same problem existed: there weren't enough teachers! There also weren't enough students—at that point our youth group had dwindled down to zero.

I realized how ponderous the trellises had become when one class told me they had been meeting for several years even though their teacher no longer attended our church. What had they been doing all that time? Watching videos, some with quite questionable theology. The trellis held more importance than vine work.

Finally, there was the unofficial but influential power group. This group nearly ended my days at Audubon Park. Apart from the grace of God, I would have bailed long ago. But reflecting on this unsanctioned group's dominance over the church's life reminds me of the importance of having a biblical leadership model. Without a biblical trellis in place, the void of leadership will be filled in unhealthy ways, inevitably neglecting essential vine work.

A Leaking Ship

As I navigated the waters of those early years, you can imagine how overwhelmed I felt. It was like we were trying to keep a leaky ship from sinking. We could see water coming in through the holes, and we knew that simply throwing it back out wasn't going to work. We had to plug the gaping holes. I felt the weight of all this. It seemed like the church would fail if I failed to maintain its multiplying structures.

If you go to a church in need of revitalization, you'll likely find something similar to what I found. Or maybe you've pastored a church for a long time and helped create unwieldy trellises. In some cases, your church's trellises may even be significantly out of line with Scripture. Whatever the situation, discipleship will suffer. But it doesn't have to stay that way. How do you lead a church to change its ecclesiological structure to better align with Scripture's teaching? This question plagued me.

So, of course, I talked with Phil. His counsel prevented a quick implosion. I was eager, energetic, and confident I had at least some of the right answers. But I needed to channel my zeal in the proper direction and press for change at a God-honoring pace. I saw a list of things that needed to change: the church's leadership structure, the role of deacons, and the membership process, just to name a few. I wanted everything to be transformed overnight!

Thankfully, Phil's counsel steered me in a biblical direction: *Pastor for longevity with biblical reform in view.*

 Mentor Phil Offers Counsel

Quite honestly, when I first began pastoral ministry, I gave little thought to longevity. My generation tended to think about moving up the ministerial ladder rather than putting down deep roots. The last thirty-plus years has changed my perspective. In my briefer pastorates, I found it difficult to develop and sustain maturity. Generally speaking, it takes a long view of pastoral ministry to pull off healthy, biblical reform.

Thinking about Shepherds

These days, it's hard to come across an actual shepherd in the wild. I've seen a few during international trips. Their jobs are hard and unrelenting. No matter the weather conditions, the terrain, or the shepherd's disposition on a particular day, the sheep always need shepherding. They need shepherds who will feed them and care for them by recognizing sickness, retrieving them from danger, protecting them from predators, and aiding in their birth. Shepherds must be diligent, attentive, and tireless in caring for the flock entrusted to them.

That's why it's the perfect biblical image for the office of pastor. The image shows up all over Scripture: from the moment aged Jacob called the Lord "my shepherd all my life long" (Genesis 48:15), to God's call for David to be a king who was "shepherd of my people Israel" (2 Samuel 5:2), to the Lord's promise to his people that "I will give you shepherds after my own heart, who will feed you with knowledge and understanding" (Jeremiah 3:15), and to the Good Shepherd who "lays down his life for his sheep" (John 10:11). Ultimately, the Bible narrows the use of the term to those the Good Shepherd entrusts with care for his flock.[3] I've never used the title *Shepherd Phil*, but it would be appropriate based on passages like 1 Peter 5:2, Acts 20:28, and Ephesians 4:11. To lose sight of the biblical pattern for shepherding the flock inevitably establishes unhealthy patterns in both a pastor and his congregation.

A Critical Passion

During the late 1990s I preached through Colossians, and the Lord deeply shook me when I got to Colossians 1:28–29. After working through the majestic Christological passage that comes before these verses, I came to the succinct aim Paul held as his ministry passion: "Him we proclaim, warning everyone and teaching everyone with all wisdom, that we may present everyone mature in Christ. For this I toil, struggling with all his energy that he powerfully works within me" (Colossians 1:28–29). The sentence emphatically begins with "*Him* we proclaim." Jesus Christ is the focus of our shepherding work—not building pretty or even functioning trellises. In other words, to the degree our church programs, buildings, budgets, committees, traditions, age-related activities, special events, crowd-gathering programs, and other trellises draw attention away from the centrality of Jesus Christ, they prove to be distractions at best and idols at worst. The aim in proclaiming Christ is to "present everyone mature in Christ." Paul's passion was to see those under his spiritual care brought to spiritual maturity. Consequently, he labored with that passion in mind.

Pastors must follow suit. They must be spurred on by Paul's vision for presenting a maturing people to the Lord of the church.

Pastoral Impatience

Christian maturity is slow, tedious work. A two-year-old isn't ready to trim the hedges or do geometry homework or apply for an after-school job. But we know that her maturity will advance if she's appropriately fed, protected, taught, and shown what maturity looks like.

And yet, too many pastors are in a rush. They presume their members have the maturity to sustain them through the adversities of life, so they make lots of changes early in ministry. But expecting an immature congregation to endure many changes is like putting a kid with a learner's permit behind the wheel of a Ferrari. Dangerous!

My dad could grow just about anything, including grapes. He knew how to prune the vines, and what kind of trellis they needed to sustain the best health and produce the most fruit. Do you know what I never saw him do? I never saw him launch in with a handful of tools and tear down the trellises while the vines were still clinging to them. He would remove portions of a trellis only after carefully making sure the vine would be sustained.

Unfortunately, some impatient pastors ruin good vines by too hastily tearing out unnecessary trellises. In almost every case, crashing into a church and suddenly chopping down long-held structures will leave vine work in jeopardy. That doesn't mean unhealthy trellises should stay forever. Eventually, they must go. But they must be strategically dismantled rather than ripped out in one fell swoop.

I ran into an odd trellis early in ministry. The church auditorium had two very worn-out boards on the wall with faded numbers and letters. These faded numbers and letters identified the weekly giving and the weekly attendance at the various church events (Sunday school and training union). To say they were unattractive and distracting understates their appearance. But they were trellises that some in the congregation cared about far more than what the trellises were supposed to be accomplishing—discipling those in attendance. Two older ladies asked before a special event if they could take down the two boards. They were concerned their appearance would be distracting. Forty years ago, in my youthful naïveté, I distinctly remember saying, "I don't care what you do with them. You can burn them as far as I'm concerned." Well, they didn't burn them but they did take them down. Simple enough, right?

Within a few days, I found out that one man would not return to church unless the boards were returned. *Ridiculous,* I thought. *How immature!* The boards became a hot topic of discussion in the next deacons meeting. After hashing out pros and cons, and since one party wanted the boards out and another wanted them in, we decided to do what seemed most natural: vote on the boards. The night of the vote, attendance at the midweek service tripled! And when the vote tallied, It was . . . a tie.

Yes, our church stood divided over two pieces of particle board with faded numbers that never spoke a word to encourage anyone in Christ. Had I realized the angst this would create, I would have been less eager to get rid of the boards and more judicious in working through more important and substantial things. The boards could eventually be moved if I'd given attention to first things first.

Granted, some trellises need to go faster than others. Some just need repairing. A pastor must first establish enough trust through faithful shepherding—through doing real vine work—that the congregation accepts his leadership to slowly bring trellises under control so they might serve rather than take over vine work.

Pastoral Longevity

Changes seem to happen most easily when a pastor is aiming for longevity. Of course, there are exceptions. Perhaps the church can't support the pastor's family; perhaps there's limited potential to serve the community bi-vocationally; perhaps major theological differences become unavoidable; perhaps unresolved personal and/or cultural differences become insurmountable. But generally speaking, pastors should approach a church's call to stay as a long-term call. These pastors may not spend their entire ministries in that first church. I certainly didn't, due to some of the reasons above. And yet, it proves helpful when pastors can approach a call with this long-run mindset.

What specifically should pastors do as they aim at the long term? Here are a few ideas:

1. Develop good listeners and interpreters of Scripture through faithfully preaching and teaching God's Word. If we give attention to Christ-centered exposition of God's Word, we not only help the church to listen well, but we also teach them how to properly handle Scripture.

2. Lead the church to make reading a priority. First, lead them to read God's Word daily. We challenge our congregation to read through the Bible yearly. Not everyone does so, but many do, while others will read much larger portions than they ever have. Second, challenge them to read good Christian works. Study books together. We do this on Wednesday nights and in small group gatherings. Pick readable, useful books, and then lead the church in finding encouragement through Christian devotional material, theology, biographies, church history, etc. Reading changes the church's perspective. Reading helps the church understand what a healthy congregation looks like and how Christian ministry takes place.

3. Disciple and train the men and women of the church. Pastors need to disciple men. Godly women need to disciple other women. These discipling relationships will bring healthy change in the church. Instead of the pastor making all the changes, many changes will arise from within the structure of maturing, godly men whom the Lord will raise up as congregational leaders. Women growing in Christ will support these healthy changes, cultivating an atmosphere of spiritual growth where the congregation desires to join in worship, mission, and service.

4. Allow changes to naturally flow from your preaching and teaching ministry. You don't need to manipulate change under the guise of preaching. Just preach the Word. The Word reveals the very changes that need to happen. The

Word dismantles far more trellises than pastoral scheming can achieve, and without the same carnage.

5. Make changes slowly. The first couple of years are about the first couple of years, not about creating major changes. Let those first two years be a time to gain the trust of those you're learning to love and shepherd. Pastors know far less about their congregations in the first two years than they realize. There's depth where it may be least expected, and there's shallowness where they first thought they would find depth.

Generally speaking, start making gradual changes in the third year and beyond. Please, don't pull out a wrecking ball at that point, thinking that after three years you can do whatever you desire. Rather, by that point you've started to love the congregation with more depth and shepherd them with more tenderness. Be sensitive to the incremental adjustments that the church *really* needs. Learn to tell the difference between trellises that need to be adjusted and trellises that need to go. Do so wisely and patiently.[4]

Most of all, pastors, don't forget this: In everything, Jesus is our model. He showed compassion to those who were like sheep without a shepherd. A pastor may not spend his life in his first pastorate, but he should make sure that whenever he leaves, the congregation is in much better shape for the man who follows him.

 Young Pastor Rich Applies the Counsel

After my conversation with Phil, one word left a lasting impression: *teach, teach, teach.* Phil told me, "Before making any changes, layer teaching with more teaching on that particular subject." One sermon and one discipleship meeting and one book study simply won't create a climate receptive to change. God's pace is usually slower than ours. So we must exercise patience. When we do, growth in maturity will come from the Lord. It will be the result of patient teaching. Phil's advice to allow changes to naturally flow from your preaching and teaching is counsel I discovered to be true.

Unfortunately, I learned this the hard way.

Somewhere around year two, I made one of the missteps Phil warned against. *I moved too quickly.* In short, I wanted to change our Wednesday evening prayer meeting. You might ask, "Why change a prayer meeting? Prayer is essential to the life and health of a local church." I agree! But . . . a prayer meeting also actually needs to be a prayer meeting.

What we called a "prayer meeting" was essentially a time for the church to eat a meal together (good), a time for teaching the Word (good), and a time for one closing prayer (not good, if your aim is to have a real prayer meeting). So in my youthful zeal, I made the decision to turn our prayer meeting into, well, a prayer meeting. Ironically, I didn't pray much about this change. I thought it would be received well. The plan was for us to eat, fellowship, and then move to a smaller room where we could pray aloud for thirty to forty-five minutes. About forty of us met in a gymnasium, and a smaller room seemed more appropriate for prayer. But two significant factors didn't cross my mind: *age* and *time.* *Age.* The members who came on Wednesday evenings were primarily in their eighties and nineties. A long walk to another room in another building took a significant amount of effort for some of them. That was poor judgment on my part, and showed a lack of pastoral care. Looking back, I didn't appreciate enough that our elderly members were even coming on

Wednesday evenings. I should have taken a posture of encouragement rather than correction. As I pressed forward with the change, I discovered that as some made the move to the prayer room, others made their way home.

Time. Put simply, I didn't give enough time to teach on the importance of prayer. Before I knew it, Wednesday evenings dropped from forty in attendance to about fifteen. In hindsight, I should have left the structure alone and simply called it a Bible study. The trellis in place was actually quite good. The church enjoyed a meal together and sat under the teaching of God's Word. But I grew impatient and didn't give enough time for the Word to do the work. A Wednesday night prayer meeting that might be misnamed isn't such a bad trellis.

If you're a pastor, let me encourage you: keep faithfully and patiently shepherding the flock. Lean on the power of the Word and prayer. As you do, God will transform both you and your congregation. Ultimately, that's what he intends. God is conforming us all to the image of his Son. Fellow pastor, pastor for longevity with biblical reform in view.

 Mentor Phil Lists Some Next Steps

- Work on teaching and preaching so that your congregation learns how to listen to biblical exposition and read the Word with more insight and fruitfulness.
- Look for ways to encourage a culture of reading good books. Provide copies of shorter books for the congregation. Develop a small book stall to allow the congregation to see useful titles to purchase. Encourage a few men and women to start a reading group. A possible starting point might be individual articles from

the *9Marks Journal* that you can download and print at no cost. Reading a short article can lead to a small book and then to books with lengthier treatments of important subjects.

- Discipling isn't always done in a structured setting. Recognize the organic ways that discipling happens with accountability, prayer, sermon discussions, and just generally encouraging one another's walk with Christ.
- Patiently allow the exposition of God's Word to do the significant work of changing minds about crusty, worn-out structures. Let the Word do the work by the Spirit. Preach and pray.

Recommended Reading

Check out the 9Marks Building Healthy Churches series of fourteen books that covers a wide range of subjects. They provide bulk purchase discounts. 9Marks Ministries also has a series of small booklets on church health in its Church Questions series. These booklets take about an hour to read and are ideal for getting the congregation accustomed to reading Christian works. The Gospel Coalition has a series of booklets edited by D. A. Carson and Timothy Keller, published by Crossway, on various doctrinal subjects (www.tgc.org). New Growth Press has a series of minibooks on counseling issues that can be made available as giveaway materials (https://new growthpress.com/minibooks/). We have found them to be excellent tools to get people thinking biblically on important subjects. Also consider the book referred to throughout this chapter, *The Trellis and the Vine: The Ministry Mind-Shift That Changes Everything*, by Colin Marshall and Tony Payne. And for more on how the pastoral (shepherding) office works out in the life of the church, see the 9Marks book *Elders in the Life of the Church*, which Phil coauthored with Matt Schmucker.

Part 3

The Tumultuous Years

Indeed, we felt that we had received
the sentence of death. But that was to make us rely
not on ourselves but on God who raises the dead.

2 Corinthians 1:9

5.

Trust the Word to Minimize or Convert

 **Young Pastor Rich Faces a Challenge**

I had read Isaiah 55:10–11 many times:

> "For as the rain and the snow come down from
> heaven
>   and do not return there but water the earth,
> making it bring forth and sprout,
>   giving seed to the sower and bread to the eater,
> so shall my word be that goes out from my mouth;
>   it shall not return to me empty,
> but it shall accomplish that which I purpose,
>   and shall succeed in the thing for which I sent it."

I knew this text by heart. I studied it in context. I prayed it back to God. But how would this work out in my ministry? Would it mean that my faithful preaching would cause the unconverted to get saved, the wayward to return to the Lord, and the saints to mature?

As Isaiah penned these words, I wonder if he pondered the moment God called him to serve as a prophet. In Isaiah 6:8, after the Lord cleansed Isaiah's guilt, he said, "Whom shall I send, and who will go for us?" Isaiah responded, "Here am I! Send me." Only then did he learn God's assignment, "Go, and say to this people: 'Keep on hearing, but do not understand; keep on seeing, but do not perceive'" (v. 9). This command perplexed him. Here was the word of God that he gave Isaiah to preach. Would God's word have a hardening effect on the unregenerate? Isaiah responded, "How long, O Lord?" (v. 11). In other words, "Is this really your purpose? I thought your word would not return empty!"

I draw attention to this text to demonstrate how God alone sets the agenda for his redemptive work. His word will achieve his redemptive purposes, even though it may appear otherwise to us. The passage in Isaiah goes on to show that God saved a remnant, but many rejected his word. Isaiah was called to be faithful no matter the result.

Pastors must learn this lesson. We must trust that as we seek to faithfully say what God has said, as we explain the text's intended meaning, his word will accomplish what he purposes. But it may not end with the results we desire.

I remember trying to lead Audubon Park toward a more biblical model of corporate worship. I hoped to incorporate more elements prescribed by Scripture. For example, Paul instructed to the church in Ephesus to be "addressing one another in psalms and hymns and spiritual songs, singing and making melody to the Lord with all your heart" (Ephesians 5:19). Clearly, congregational singing is the primary form of singing when the church gathers.[1] Yet, much of our music focused on "special music" that the congregation listened to rather than sing. As I taught on this subject, I was confident God's Word would accomplish its purpose. But I had no idea what that purpose would be! As it turned out, we experienced some tumultuous years as we initially grappled with our approach to worship and other areas of ministry. But over time, God's Word shaped not only how we sing. We've also incorporated a call to worship, prayers of confession and thanksgiving, pastoral prayers, and Scripture readings.

Leading with the Word of God

As you aim to faithfully lead with the ministry of the Word through preaching, teaching, leading members' meetings or committee meetings, counseling, and discipleship, you will discover that, for some, a renewed emphasis on biblical instruction is refreshing. For others, however, it will be unwelcome. Both marked my experience.

Over the course of the first three or four years, I tried hard to let the Word of God guide us in every area of church life. In addition to corporate worship, I also taught on church polity and governance, church membership, discipleship, prayer, missions, church discipline, and other important subjects. Sometimes this happened in settings where I could focus on certain topics, such as during a Sunday morning class. I also tried to address them in my preaching whenever the texted allowed for it. I made plenty of blunders; for example, I was impatient. But through it all, I focused on making the Word of God primary when we gathered for worship and in smaller settings. I noticed some people gravitating toward the teaching of Scripture and others toward the traditions of the church.

The Word Received

Here's what I discovered. If a pastor commits himself and his ministry to God's Word, he'll find some will gladly receive it. In John 10:3, Jesus says of the Good Shepherd, "The sheep hear his voice, and he calls his own sheep by name and leads them out." The Good Shepherd awakens us from death to eternal life through his Word. This is the effectual call of God. *He calls his own sheep by name.* Then the Good Shepherd sanctifies us through his Word. *He leads them out.* Put simply, God's people will gladly receive the Good Shepherd's Word.

As an example, we started to meet in small groups on Sunday evenings. We discussed the passage of Scripture from that morning and tried to apply it to our lives. In those smaller groups, I discovered church members who hungered and thirsted for God's Word. They wanted to follow him into green pastures, and so his Word was gladly received.

As I continued to teach the Word, more questions arose. For example, I taught through the book of Acts for about two years. I naturally addressed many issues related to evangelism and missions. Countless times in small group settings, discussion took off around these subjects. People wanted to learn how to make disciples! Why? Because they believed in the life-giving power of gospel! They believed Christ was and is the risen Lord. They heard the Good Shepherd's voice through the Word of God and wanted more nourishment. This shouldn't have surprised me. No matter where we teach it, we should expect God's people to *desire* God's Word. His Word does not return void.

The Word Rejected

If only ministry were always that encouraging! If a pastor commits himself and his ministry to God's Word, then he'll also find that some will not receive it. Maybe you've ministered to a particular couple or an individual for months, even years. And it just appears that the Word isn't taking root. In fact, in some cases it may be rejected outright.

One memory stands out. After counseling a man for a few weeks, I remember him finally looking at me and saying, "Are we just going to keep looking at what the Bible says?" He never returned. Some church members don't want the Word because they're happy with what's comfortable or familiar or just plain easy. Every pastor faces obstacles like these.

The Word Unites and Minimizes

As you seek to faithfully minister the Word of God, you'll discover it both unites and divides. What do you do when this happens? How do you know if you've caused the division, or if God is at work? This isn't an easy matter to discern.

I talked with Phil about this. And his counsel may surprise you. Here's what he told me: "The Word of God both converts and minimizes." In other words, the gospel transforms some and minimizes the influence of others who oppose gospel ministry. So, he said, be faithful and let God do the work.

 Mentor Phil Offers Counsel

We say we believe "Only the Word" when it comes to life and ministry. We're passionate about the Bible. We read it, pray it, preach it, and discuss it. But do we depend on God's Word when it comes to how we conduct our ministry?

I join you in the confession, Only the Word. I would have said that from the start of my ministry. Yet too often, sometimes without realizing it, I slipped into patterns where I depended more on my gifts or my personality or some new idea floating around evangelical circles to bring about change in the congregation. A few times, I found myself trying to find the next greatest idea or method for ministry. To be painfully honest, I hoped that I would discover it, become famous, and experience financial independence. Maybe you've been there— or maybe you *are* there.

About seven years into pastoral ministry, then in my third pastorate, I knew there had to be a better way. I attended a few conferences, got a little inspiration, tried some ideas, and saw a little movement in the church. After a huge leap, I decided to do a Doctor of Ministry degree in church growth from a well-known seminary that had originated the term and produced most of the books. I plunged myself into reading, writing, and attending seminars. I became enamored with the *certainty* that if I put into practice the *axioms* and *principles* taught in these seminars, then I could almost guarantee that I would be pastoring a church like the ones I read about. I researched large, growing churches. I interviewed pastors who had seemingly arrived. Then I would go back to my small-town, sickly church and attempt to put some of these new ideas into practice.

But the longer I sat through the seminars and read the books, the more disenchanted I became. It wasn't that the presentations lacked verve or the books failed to inspire. The problem, as I finally began to *think theologically*, was just how atheological and often unbiblical so many of these axioms and principles appeared to be. I began to realize that many things presented as biblical ideas were no more than sociological observations couched with a little Bible to add credibility.

I faced a crisis in ministry. Would I go the direction of the church growth movement with its strategies based on sociology and marketing? Or would I go back to the foundation for life and ministry—Only the Word?

I planted a church in the middle of my doctoral work, which meant I could field test some of these principles. But slowly, I began to see the inside of the church in ways I'd never noticed. I looked at some churches that appeared impressive statistically, but their staffs did not get along, or their pastors did not shepherd, or they mastered opening wide the front door of the church while doing nothing to close the back door. I knew that bloated membership rolls didn't fit the biblical pattern for church membership. Pastoral staff infighting didn't manifest an example for the flock. And the preaching came across as superficial, almost as a necessary element to keep the ecclesiastical machinery going but in no way central to the life of the church. Worship services focused on entertaining rather than unleashing hearts in grateful worship and praise.

And then it hit me: I was heading in the same direction.

The one thing that kept my feet on the ground was a commitment I had made when I was a junior in college, once I first sensed the stirrings of the Spirit to pastor. Way back then I committed myself to an expositional ministry. Much of what I had studied about church growth did not square with what I kept seeing in the Bible. I finally realized: the Word had to do the work by the Spirit. Otherwise, whatever's happening won't last. And so, once again, *Only the Word* became my passion for ministry. But this time, it stuck.

Why Only the Word?

Think about it. How do we know what the church is or how the church functions apart from the Word of God? There's a reason the Reformation reclaimed *sola scriptura*. More than anything, this moment in church history sought to tether the church back to its intended foundation—Christ and his Word. *Sola scriptura* became the rallying cry to break the iron grip of Roman Catholicism on the Western world. Of course, not every Reformer agreed at every point! Just like us, they interpreted various doctrines and practices differently, leading to differing traditions. But the same impulse undergirded them all: only the Word could direct and assure the church of the Lord Jesus.

So how do we know if we're actually depending on the Word above all else? The real test is whether or not we are making it central in our pastoral work and church life. Consider these questions as a litmus test:

- Do we go to God's Word to understand what the church is and what it should look like (for example, a passage like Ephesians 5:22–32)?
- Do we go to God's Word to understand how the church functions as the people of God (passages like Ephesians 4:1–16; 1 Peter 2:1–12)?
- Do we go to God's Word to understand who leads the church, how it makes decisions, and who can be counted as part of the body (passages like 1 Peter 5:1–5; Acts 15:6–29; Matthew 18:15–20)?
- Do we go to God's Word to understand how the church gathers, serves one another, and scatters into the world on mission (passages like Hebrews 10:19–25; 1 Thessalonians 5:11–22; Titus 2:1–15; Matthew 28:18–20; 1 Peter 2:9–10)?
- How do we know what kind of character we need in pastors and deacons leading the church, apart from the Word's declaration (passages like 1 Timothy 3:1–13; Titus 1:5–9)? How do we know the responsibilities entrusted to those shepherding the flock apart from

the Word (passages like Acts 6:1–7; 20:28; 2 Timothy 4:1–5; 1 Peter 5:1–5; Hebrews 13:17)?

- How do we understand what the local church is to look like or how its members are to relate to one another or what constitutes a breach in membership calling for discipline, apart from the Word (passages like Ephesians 2:19–22; 4:1–5:21; Romans 12:1–13; 1 Corinthians 5:1–13; 12:1–14:40; Matthew 18:15–20; Galatians 5:1–5; Titus 3:9–11)?
- Do we go to God's Word for the sanctification of the flock (John 17:17)?

Even if the only portion of the Word we possessed was the Epistles, we would find answers to all these questions. But we have much more! The whole of God's Word guides the church and its pastors into living as the people of God.

Depending on the Word Leads to Trusting in the Lord

Rich has already reminded us of how the Word goes forth to accomplish God's purpose. The Lord directs the Word to be planted and bear good fruit to his glory: "It shall not return to me empty, but it shall accomplish that which I purpose, and shall succeed in the thing for which I sent it" (Isaiah 55:11). David sang of the Word (using synonyms: law, testimony, precepts, commandments, fear, judgments):

> The Law of the LORD **is perfect,** restoring the soul;
> The testimony of the LORD **is sure,** making wise the simple.
> The precepts of the LORD **are right,** rejoicing the heart;

The commandment of the LORD **is pure,** enlighten-
ing the eyes.

The fear of the LORD **is clean,** enduring forever;
The judgments of the LORD **are true;** they are righ-
teous altogether.

They are more desirable than gold, yes, than much
pure gold;

Sweeter also than honey and drippings of the
honeycomb.

Moreover, Your servant is warned by them;
In keeping them there is great reward. (Psalm 19:7–
11 NASB)

With rhythmic beauty, David declares that the Word is
perfect and sure, simple and pure, clean and true. It encompasses the most intense desires, it delights the highest tastes,
it warns and rewards. It lasts while programs, gimmicks, and
ideas change with the wind. "The grass withers, the flower
fades, but the word of our God will stand forever" (Isaiah 40:8).

Luther famously was asked how he brought about the reformation of the church. He didn't do it, he confessed. God did
it through his Word. Luther just taught the Word while the
Spirit did the reforming work.

How Do We Let the Word Do the Work?

1. Preach well. We've talked about this already. Trust the
power, clarity, and authority of the Word to uproot problem
issues, change recalcitrant people, move aside those given to
divisiveness, and bring health to the church by the Spirit's
inward application.

2. Pray consistently. Jesus gave us the example. Even when busy with ministry, he withdrew to pray, for he depended upon the Spirit to work through the proclamation of the Word. Systematically pray through your members by name (I recommend doing so every week unless your church size makes it unwieldy). Pray for the gatherings; pray through the sermon in preparation and even while delivering; pray for the mission and service of the church.

3. Shepherd the flock with the Word. Whether you are preaching or visiting members or doing hospital visits or counseling or sitting with those grieving their loss, let the Word permeate your shepherding. Leave your people with the Word instead of your cleverness. Model for them how the Word affects your daily walk. Often, something in my morning devotional will be just what I need. On those occasions, the Lord gives me a chance not only to serve them through the Word but to model the aim of helping them learn to live in the Word.

4. Wait on the Lord. The Lord owns his Word. And the church belongs to him. He bought it at great price. Even the gates of Hades will not prevail against Jesus's church (Matthew 16:18). He will work as he pleases. Meanwhile, we learn to trust him to do what we cannot do. Refuse to bow to manipulation or twisting the truth. *Only the Word.*

5. Stay at the wheel. Don't give up. Too many pastors never see the beautiful fruit of a Word-focused ministry because they grow impatient and leave. Enjoy the process. I'm serious. Hard days will come, but take heart. The Lord of the church hones and shapes his undershepherds so that we might be more useful in shepherding his flock. Throughout, we discover more and more the power of the Word of God transforming the people we're trying to shepherd toward being formed in the image of Christ.

 ## Young Pastor Rich Applies the Counsel

Culture shifts don't happen overnight. I continually remind myself of this reality. But when the culture at Audubon Park began to noticeably shift to an Only the Word–focused ministry, I felt something in my own soul: *rest*. When pastors and congregations rely on the Word of God, eagerness to keep up with other flourishing churches dissipates. In fact, new desires arise. You find yourself thanking God as other churches thrive. You regularly pray for them to bear gospel fruit. You realize that as God does his work through his Word, it helps us take on a kingdom mindset that gladly acknowledges that the work is bigger than us. God uses all his churches, and that's worth celebrating.

Looking back, I'm most grateful that Phil taught me the lesson to wait on the Lord. A Word-focused ministry leaves the results up to God. This takes a great burden off the pastor and the congregation. In our evangelism, we turn to the Word. As we pray over and organize mission endeavors, we turn to the Word. Structuring worship gatherings? We turn to the Word. And even when a church apparently divides over the Word, *we turn to the Word*. If a church makes a habit of seeking God's instruction for all matters through his Word, then when problems or challenges arise, everyone's attention turns in the same direction. What does the Word of God say?

I remember inviting someone to attend a worship service at Audubon Park a couple of years ago. He seemed interested. I told him something he found odd: "Prepare to be unimpressed."

Was that the most encouraging thing to say? Probably not. But my point was that there are no gimmicks, no attractions, no efforts to hook anyone who visits. We're just a bunch of sinners in need of redemption by a great Savior who is revealed through . . . the Word.

Mentor Phil Lists Some Next Steps

- Listen to at least one biblical exposition from a faithful expositor each week for the next two months. How do they handle the text? How do they apply it to the congregation? How does their preaching demonstrate confidence in God's Word?
- Read sermons by some of the faithful pastors of past generations like Charles Haddon Spurgeon, Samuel Davies, Andrew Fuller, Charles Simeon, John Calvin, Martin Luther, Jonathan Edwards, J. A. Alexander, Martyn Lloyd-Jones, or any number of Puritans (such as John Bunyan, Thomas Brooks, Thomas Watson, Richard Sibbes). Soak in the way they handled the Word and applied it to their congregations.
- Read biographies of pastors who depended on God's Word to do the work in their churches. Any biographies of pastors noted above will be worth reading.

Recommended Reading

Preaching and Preachers by D. Martyn Lloyd-Jones

On Preaching: Personal and Pastoral Insights for the Preparation and Practice of Preaching by H. B. Charles Jr.

The Art of Prophesying by William Perkins

6.

Should I Stay? Follow Jesus's Model

👥 Young Pastor Rich Faces a Challenge

Woodworking rewards the patient craftsman. My dad had good woodworking skills. One year a tornado passed through our community and blew down a maple tree that sat in the corner lot of my childhood home. My dad took the tree to a sawmill, had it cut into manageable pieces, and then began to craft a bassinet for his grandchildren. He designed, shaped, sanded, stained, and assembled the raw wood until a beautiful piece of furniture emerged. It took patient and attentive work before he was rewarded with the finished product.

Unlike the craftsman's work, pastoral ministry is not so consistently rewarding. When a pastor longs to see the fruit of his labors, he often discovers that his work is never really done. After laboring for revitalization at Audubon Park for five years, I thought I had killed the church. Sure, I saw fruit in a few individuals' lives. The gospel gave hope to a number of members. I observed glimpses of grace: a deeper hunger for God's Word, a culture of hospitality, a willingness to serve in the least glamorous ways. But what became most evident was the brewing division in the life of the church. That division blinded me from seeing the good fruit before my eyes.

It came to a head at a regularly scheduled members meeting following the worship service. Before my wife and I went into that meeting, we sincerely thought it would be our last Sunday. At that time, any member could make a motion, have it seconded, and the church vote to approve. I thought the church would vote to remove me as senior pastor.

After two and a half hours of accusations (mostly incredulous, with an occasional kernel of credibility), a very influential member of the church stood up and began with these words: "I've never lost a motion in this church. I was going to make a motion that we fire you today. But instead, I just want to ask that you and your family move on."

I responded, "With all due respect, unless the church says otherwise, we plan to stay." After that, no one else had anything to say. The meeting ended abruptly. Discouragement dogged us the next few weeks.

By God's grace, several members encouraged us as we haltingly walked through the next season at Audubon Park. Despite the encouragement, the atmosphere left me in a fog. Instead of looking at the flock and seeing precious souls, I saw numbers. And they were low. Really low. It seemed like every week the attendance declined. Most naturally, I began to question whether it was time for us to leave. Had I caused the church to implode? Did I do more harm than good?

Is It Time to Leave?

A pastor may find himself in an especially discouraging season of ministry. That's not unusual. I tried so hard to lead the church toward revitalization through preaching, praying, and shepherding with the Word. Before coming, I envisioned new conversions, elders installed, deacons serving, multi-generational and multi-ethnic growth, visible unity, and a church filled with passion for the gospel to reach the nations. Instead, I felt as though I had crashed a plane with everyone on board.

I remember calling Phil and asking his advice: "When will I know if it's time to leave?" The counsel he gave pierced my heart and convinced me that it wasn't time to go.

Now, before I share his counsel, I want to preface what I'm about to say. I don't want to suggest that if a pastor leaves a church, he isn't a good undershepherd. In fact, leaving may be the most God-honoring thing to do in certain situations. But this very point highlights the need for godly mentors. Phil knew my family and me well. He had walked with me and our church through five years of ministry. He knew the intricacies of our situation.

And so he pointed me to a single verse, John 10:15. Jesus says, "I lay down my life for the sheep." Once I heard those words, I resolved that I could not leave during such a tumultuous time. There were sheep who desired the Word of God and wanted to be discipled. Phil pointed to Jesus as the Good Shepherd who gave his life as the ultimate sacrifice for his sheep. But Jesus is also an example for those he appoints to shepherd his flock. I knew the road ahead was uncertain. I wasn't sure anyone would show up for corporate worship. Would we even be able to pay the utility bills? To say I was discouraged is an understatement. But the Holy Spirit patiently taught me the importance of sacrifice for the good of God's people.

Too often, our natural default is to leave. I know it was mine.

Maybe you're asking the same question: *When will I know it's time to leave?* At the very least, I would ask you to meditate on this biblical counsel and look to Jesus as the chief example of faithful pastoral ministry. "I lay down my life for the sheep."

Mentor Phil Offers Counsel

I remember Rich's phone call. The members meeting loomed. So did opposition by a few longstanding, outspoken members. I heard the heartache in his voice and sensed the desperation of the moment. What would happen? I texted him this note just a couple weeks before the showdown:

> Remember that they would like to put you in a position to resign. Of course, they would like for you to do that spontaneously. Do not make that easy for them. You are the pastor, so stand boldly upon the Word and continue on. I meditated this morning from the end of Ephesians 3. God's power is at work in his church to display his glory. What hinders it? Chapter 4 indicates a failure to walk worthy and disunity. Praying that APBC will see that and not balk.

I loved how Rich responded to my note: "I think through all of this the Lord has brought me to the end of myself, so I'll fully rest in him." That's what happens in trials. We finally start to look away from ourselves and rest in the Lord. When pastoral ministry goes smoothly, it's easy to rely upon our abilities. Only when things get unsettled do we realize we've never been a good foundation upon which to build our ministry.

Two weeks later, I waited for word from Rich on how the meeting went. "Just got out. Still pastor of APBC," he texted. Despite the opposition and intimidation, the Lord sustained him as the church's pastor. Here's the amazing thing: most of the congregation loved him! It may have taken a painful church meeting to make it clear, but his stance on behalf of the church he loved and longed to shepherd changed the direction for the future. He didn't know what would happen over the next few weeks, but he knew he intended to remain as the shepherd of this little flock who loved the Lord and their pastor.

A Few *Givens*

Not every stressful members meeting has a happy ending. Sometimes pastors get fired. Sometimes churches split. Still other times a stalemate continues with a power group waiting for the pastor to get tired of the grumbling and move on. As Rich mentioned earlier, sometimes the pastor does need to move. But probably more often than we realize, he needs to stay. The future health of the church may rest on the courageous stand of a pastor who will not give in to opponents' threats.

Let's consider a few *givens* in this regard:

1. Given, not every church and pastor make a good fit. Candidating for a church may leave neither church nor pastor the wiser. A two-page biographical sketch, an online sermon, a couple of short articles, and a weekend visit tell the congregation a little about the prospective pastor. From the other angle, conversations with the search committee, looking over the latest iteration of a constitution, and a weekend visit can't satisfy the prospective pastor's understanding of exactly what he's getting into. He may lack the skills to serve that church. The church may lack the cohesiveness to follow that pastor's ministry. Their personalities may clash. His gifts may be too strong or too weak. The church's desires may run counter to his pastoral aims. In such cases, leaving might be best. If the church, after a reasonable attempt, will not accept the pastor's shepherding skills and aims, then he may need to peaceably pursue another flock and they another shepherd.

2. Given, not every pastor fits into the church's ethos and community. Every church has its own bent. Certain things interest them. A style of music and worship may be so engrained in their thinking that to consider otherwise brings massive conflict. The community, especially smaller communities or deeply entrenched suburban areas, may have their own version of how churches ought to function and what role pastors ought to play. If they have an attitude that he's an outsider and will never let him in, then a pastor will have difficulty remaining for long despite his best efforts. He can try to meld into the local ethos: cheering on the high school teams, shopping locally, supporting the middle school cheerleaders' car wash, or offering an invocation at the aldermen meetings. He may try for months, then years. If he's still an outsider tolerated by the locals while not really heeding his pastoral ministry, then it may be best to find another congregation for long-term ministry.

3. Given, not every church responds well to their pastor's best efforts. When a pastor begins, he must do so with the intention of building on what other pastors have done before him. He must seek to discern how well the church understands and applies the gospel, how well they grasp the nature of the church, and how focused they are on the church's mission. It could be that previous pastors have done little to facilitate gospel, ecclesiological, and missiological understanding. In such a case, he will need to patiently lay groundwork that should have already existed. Some churches respond with joy at this foundation-laying work. Other churches lurch. They prefer something else to biblical Christianity, and they probably don't realize it. They want the pastor to dedicate the babies, marry the young couples, bury the dead, and beyond that, stay out of their lives. In such cases, after a reasonable time of plowing, sowing, and cultivating the church, if they show no responsiveness he may need to find another place of ministry.

Probably most pastors have thought of leaving their post. But *thoughts* must always be taken to the Word and examined by prayer. If they continue, the pastor should seek counsel from faithful pastors who know him and understand something of his ministry setting. Then, when the peace of the Lord settles in, he must be decisive whether he stays or goes.

In one church I served, the ministry seemed to be moving along rather well. Attendance was steady. Giving increased. Fellowship strengthened. While a few problems arose here and there, nothing major precipitated a sudden move. And yet, for a few months, I sensed that the Lord was going to move me. I had nothing to run away from. Many of the people were kind and attentive, showing appreciation for God's Word. But they showed little desire to change from the way they had conducted church for scores of years. Mission was something they did through their offerings but nothing beyond that. The semi-rural congregation stuck together and wanted little to do with those beyond the community. Their contentment with the status quo did not mesh well with my pastoral burden. I sensed the Lord releasing me from my post. After wise counsel from an older pastor, I moved on to serve another church.

A Few *Howevers*

However, pastors need not be quick to move. Pastoral work *will* create a few conflicts and difficulties. It's normal. Biblical preaching and teaching runs counter to typical thoughts and desires. Conflicts arise. Complaints get voiced. The pastor feels strained. But that may mean the Holy Spirit is at work through the ministry of the Word to uproot, change, and transform the congregation. Running from the problem at such a time will be the worst thing the pastor can do. Consider a few *howevers* that might inform our thinking:

1. However, some churches long to see sustained pastoral tenure if the pastor will only endure the conflicts and stay. Too often, churches grow accustomed to two-, three-, and four-year tenures, then the pastor moves on. Just about the time they get to know the pastor, and just about the time he's reaching a critical point of climbing over obstacles to the church's health, the pastor departs. And then they start the same process again—both church and pastor. The only way to get past the conflicts and difficulties is to stay. Battles aren't won by retreats. The adversary of the church builds strongholds in the personalities of the congregation that can only be torn down by faithful exposition and prayer (see 2 Corinthians 10:1–6). Brief pastorates fail to tear down strong barriers. Churches long for pastors to stay, serve, love, and care for them until they begin to mirror Christ.

2. However, some churches may need just a few members to leave, and they will be on the road to spiritual vitality. That was certainly the case with Rich. He did not attempt to run people off. That's not a faithful pastor's style. Instead, he gave attention to preaching God's Word and prayer, while shepherding the body toward health. Over time, through the ordinary means of grace, the Lord changed or moved out some disgruntled and divisive members. When Rich didn't back down from the threats of one power-grasping member, it broke that member's stronghold on the church. The people had cowered under his intimidation for years. They just needed a pastor to stand with them and endure.

3. However, some pastors will discover amid hard struggles the greatest rewards in pastoral work. It's so odd. Right in the middle of hard times—that's when the Lord does his best work, making himself known in power and grace. The Lord loves to work in our weakness because that's when we tend to depend upon him with more intensity. That's when we discover his faithfulness in our neediness. Only after enduring the hard times will the pastor know what the Lord meant when he told Paul, "My power is made perfect in weakness" (2 Corinthians 12:9).

4. However, some pastors need to shepherd more like Jesus who laid down his life for the sheep. Obviously, all pastors need to follow the model of the Good Shepherd who laid down his life for the sheep. That's hard to do in short pastorates. When the heat of difficulties and trials intensify, those pastors begin to understand the costliness of shepherding a people toward spiritual vitality. It will demand time and tears, discipline and courage, love and compassion. Those qualities modeled so beautifully by the Lord Jesus will not develop quickly, nor without cost. And yet, it's when pastors become more like Jesus that the message proclaimed and the example put forth begins to take root in the church.

A Plan to Consider

How should a pastor process the tug to leave or the pull to stay? Let's think about four considerations:

1. Shepherd the flock entrusted to you until you are fully convinced the Good Shepherd has released you from your charge. No doubt, that's a subjective call. So don't do it alone. Pray with others, seek godly counsel, listen to your wife's insights, and avoid hastiness. Consider taking a few days off to get away from the middle of pastoral responsibilities to reflect, pray, and meditate on the decision. You might write out a pros and cons list.

When the peace of the Lord settles your heart on moving, that's when you can move forward. While you're in the process of leaving, continue to faithfully preach God's Word, pray for the church, and shepherd them well. When peace to leave doesn't come, then dig deeper into pastoral work right where you are. The Lord might move you later, but until that time be faithful to your calling. The church may be on the verge of its best days.

2. If possible, don't let opposition and problems become the reasons for leaving. Unless it's an unusual situation, seek to leave on your own by the Lord's direction. You might later regret backing down when you could have taken a stand. Or you might wish you had been more patient in the middle of difficulties. That's why it normally seems best to be slow to move to ensure you're not running from one problem into another. The next church you serve could very well have more problems on hand! Sometimes it's best to work through the problems you're experiencing than to start all over with another set.

3. Be willing, if possible, to weather opposition to enable the church to get on level footing. Sadly, many churches have power groups. It may be one or two longstanding members who act like the church belongs to them. It may be a few families who give a lot of money and so believe themselves to be the highest shareholders. As long as such groups remain active and influential, a church will remain unsteady and turbulent. A pastor must be courageous to endure opposition as he seeks to wisely cut the cords of bondage.

4. Stay and grow along with the congregation. Learn to live life together, laughing and rejoicing, weeping and suffering, admonishing and encouraging one another. I was recently asked by some seminary students what I had learned about enduring with a congregation. I pointed to the *one another* passages in the New Testament as demonstrative of what I sought to practice and teach to my congregation. The more we practice the *one another* commands together, the more we grow together. Through this practice we discover the joy of deepening relationships and a depth of shepherding that brief pastorates will never enjoy.

Staying or leaving a pastorate, *if God wills*, calls for a willingness to stay and a willingness to leave. Otherwise, the concern is not God's will but our desires. Be hesitant to leave. Be willing to stay. Be sensitive to the Holy Spirit's prompting. Be open to surprising counsel. Fight discouragement by reminding yourself as often as you need to that the church is Christ's, not yours. And you are his undershepherd who serves at his pleasure.

Young Pastor Rich Applies the Counsel

Much uncertainty remained after the members meeting. I had no idea what God would do in the days, weeks, or months ahead. However, I was confident I needed to stay put. My wife and I both agreed that to leave at that point would have felt like disobedience. So by God's sustaining grace, we stayed.

I didn't know it at the time, but Phil's words of counsel about *growing with the congregation* would turn out to be foundational for the future years of seeing good fruit. Let's face it: all of us are broken sinners in need of Christ's redemption. What I failed to understand, primarily because of my pride, is that no amount of theological education prepares a man for pastoral ministry like the *work of actual pastoral ministry*. The apparent implosion of the church, in my mind, was a mark against my ability to lead. But God was maturing both pastor and congregation as we walked through those challenging years together.

If a pastor asks, "Should I stay?" consider this: If you plant a seed, at some point you recognize that you can't make the seed grow. God alone gives growth. But you can cultivate the area in and around the seed to foster growth. So that's what you do. You water the seeds, you remove the weeds, and you feed the soil good nutrients. And then finally, one day you notice a small sprout growing out of the ground. A burst of excitement fills your heart. But then you realize: this is only the beginning. The consistent work needed for healthy growth is taxing because weeds grow much easier than seeds.

Eventually, you grow tired and you're ready to give up. Maybe you don't realize that a battle takes place underneath the soil. The roots of the sprout and weeds fight for nutrients. As they fight to claim the jurisdiction of the soil, you have an important role. While the roots of the sprout do get stronger and grow deeper, the weeds need to be removed so the sprout can continue growing.

Here's the point. Does the gospel need help? No. God alone gives the growth. But in God's sovereign wisdom he strategically gives the church pastors to shepherd the flock toward spiritual maturity in Christ.

It may be that God wants you to cultivate the spiritual health of the church you currently shepherd. While it may not appear as though God is working, you and I can't see underneath the soil. The saints you shepherd mature in Christ through trials. And you are there to build up the saints in the faith. As you do, the battle may be exhausting. Draw help from Phil's counsel. Every farmer needs a break. So do pastors. But at least consider enduring for the sheep's benefit to see what good fruit may come, fruit you would otherwise never see.

 Mentor Phil Lists Some Next Steps

- When struggles mount, it's normal to desire to leave. Instead, seek the Lord in your spiritual disciplines. Die to selfish desires. Seek to have a willing heart to do the Lord's will. Be willing to suffer for the sake of Christ if he wills.

- Get away for at least a day or two to pray, read the Word, think through what the Lord has been doing in your pastoral work, and consider how you might best serve the flock. Rather than a default mode of leaving, think instead about staying. The Lord may turn your heart. But let him confirm through prayer, godly counsel, and patient waiting that it's time to leave.

- Staying may feel costly. Be conscious that the adversary of the church works to divide and discourage congregations and pastors. Put on the full armor of God from Ephesians 6:10–20. Consider if any of the complaints against your ministry hold a kernel of truth. If so, work on those issues (for example, if you are told you are not approachable, you preach too long, you want to change too many things). Distinguish between what Christ has commanded for his undershepherds and personal preferences or personality issues. Show humility by learning from critics. Show courage by standing on the Word.
- Stay at the helm of preaching, praying, and shepherding faithfully. Let nothing deter you from the charge Christ has given you for the church you pastor.

Recommended Reading

In Phil's book *40 Questions about Pastoral Ministry*, part 5, "The Church and Pastoral Ministry," deals more thoroughly with many of the issues raised in this chapter. Specifically, see pages 311–22 for recommendations on how to evaluate when it's time to leave a church. You also might read:

A Big Gospel in Small Places: Why Ministry in Forgotten Communities Matters by Stephen Witmer (a helpful, challenging book)

Liberating Ministry from the Success Syndrome by Kent and Barbara Hughes (for encouragement to get beyond the illusion of success)

Pastors and Their Critics: A Guide to Coping with Criticism in the Ministry by Joel Beeke and Nick Thompson (a most insightful book on handling criticism)

7.

In Desperate Moments, Live in the Gospel

 Young Pastor Rich Faces a Challenge

Here's one of the oddest verses about ministry: "Indeed, we felt that we had received the sentence of death. But that was to make us rely not on ourselves but on God who raises the dead" (2 Corinthians 1:9). Wait a second: a *sentence of death*? Remember this is from Paul, the man often regarded as the greatest example of faithfulness to Christ, Christian leadership, theological brilliance, and gospel zeal—the man who couldn't be distracted from the Great Commission. That's how he humbly explains gospel ministry. Anyone reading Paul's New Testament letters quickly learns he towered as a leader, yet only "by the grace of God" (1 Corinthians 15:10). His own power and abilities proved inadequate. He testified, "I have been crucified with Christ. It is no longer I who live, but Christ who lives in me. And the life I now live in the flesh I live by faith in the Son of God, who loved me and gave himself for me" (Galatians 2:20). His strength for every demand of life and ministry came through living a Christ-centered life.

Having introduced the "sentence of death" at the start of 2 Corinthians, Paul uses the rest of the epistle to pull back the curtain and let readers glimpse what he meant and how the sentence of death operated in his experience: excessive burdens (1:8), assaults on his integrity (1:15–18), concern for team members' welfare (2:12–13), afflictions (4:16–18), multiplied distresses and beatings and imprisonments and deprivations (6:4–5), congregational reactions (7:5–13), attacks on his apostleship (chapters 11 and 12), and his thorn in the flesh (12:7). In all these trials, he could not rescue himself. His giant intellect, extraordinary gifts, and unflagging zeal fell short. The gavel had fallen. His strength? Depleted. He despaired of life itself. So how would the great apostle respond? Here's what he learned: "But that was to make us rely not on ourselves but on God who raises the dead" (2 Corinthians 1:9). Instead of looking inward, Paul knew he must look to Christ. He stood as he kneeled. He stood in grace.

Living in the gospel of grace is a lifelong, day-by-day learning process. But in God's infinite wisdom, he often uses moments of desperation to teach us to trust him. This was (and is) certainly true of my experience. Men entering the pastorate for the first time have big dreams and big ideas. They feel like they know what the fruit of their ministry will look like. In doing so, they put the proverbial cart before the horse. I know I did, and I still battle this tendency.

But when we think this way and ministry doesn't go as we expected, we're crushed. Some pastors will despair to the point of quitting or bolting to another pastorate. Others endure but with increasing despondency and cynicism. Must it be this way?

Fruit Before the Work

Pastors, especially young ones, often have biblically informed ideas of how churches grow, what pastoral responsibilities should be, the way a church should be governed, and the best way to structure discipleship. At the same time, young pastors rarely understand that it takes time to lead a church toward these God-honoring ambitions. In other words, they expect to taste the fruit before it ripens. It's important to know the direction a church should go. But it's equally important to know that pastoral ministry generally demands patient, slow, God-dependent work.

After I resolved to stay at my church despite the effort to remove me, a question remained: "Would I now stay in my own power or learn to stay by God's grace?" The answer may seem obvious, but the reality I faced revealed a war between the flesh and the Spirit. When pastors go through tumultuous times, when it feels like the sentence of death overshadows them, they're tempted to look inward for answers. "How can I fix this?" they query. Instead, they should ask, "What is the Lord teaching me? How is he reordering my life and ministry?" Most often, the Lord uses these moments to steer us to find everyday comfort in the gospel of grace that we preach every week. Or, in Paul's language, "to rely not on ourselves, but on God who raises the dead."

When the dust settled after the difficult members meeting, we tried to see a way forward even though the issues ahead seemed insurmountable. Giving would certainly go down. Way down. Our 85,000-square-foot facility hung like an albatross around our necks. Monthly costs for building and staff far exceeded income. Would those who remained eventually leave? Would we reach the point where we couldn't open our doors because our utilities were cut off? I had been conducting funerals for a lot of older members. Would I be conducting the funeral for the church I pastored?

Personally, I was exhausted. *Discouraged, weary,* and *burned out.* But I wasn't alone. The remaining members felt the cloud of despair hanging over the church as well. Every week, someone would ask me the same exasperating question: "What are we going to do?" To be honest, I had no idea.

Depending on God

All pastors go through difficult situations. Sometimes, we don't heed James's counsel: "Count it all joy, my brothers, when you meet trials of various kinds" (James 1:2). The pain blinds us to the joy found by trusting in Christ. You may be experiencing a significant trial right now. It may seem odd, but here's what I'm continuing to learn: *In these difficult moments, God has you exactly where he wants you.*

James could count it all joy during trials because his theology aligned with Paul's. He knew that trials and hardships serve to deliver us from trusting in ourselves. No wonder James follows his call to joy with a call for wisdom: "If any of you lacks wisdom, let him ask God, who gives generously to all without reproach, and it will be given him" (1:5). It takes wisdom to learn to rely on Christ.

This may be this book's most important chapter. Why? Because if a pastor can't learn to rely on Christ through ministry's ups and downs, then he can't be a pastor for long. Once again, we emphasize the need to find a faithful pastoral mentor who has walked in your shoes, understands your ambitions, and learned to rely upon the faithfulness of Jesus Christ. This mentor may serve as God's instrument to help you learn what it means to depend upon Christ as he has learned to do.

 ## Mentor Phil Offers Counsel

Although he insisted it would never happen, Peter denied the Lord just like Jesus said he would. "Simon, Simon, behold, Satan demanded to have you, that he might sift you like wheat," Jesus foretold, "but I have prayed for you that your faith may not fail. And when you have turned again, strengthen your brothers" (Luke 22:31–32). The trial of denial would come, as would others along the way. Yet Jesus did not focus first on Peter's ministry. He focused on his faith—his conscious dependence upon the Lord Jesus who laid down his life in an atoning death to secure Peter forever. Peter's faith would not fail because Jesus did not fail. When Peter fled the high priest's courtyard after hearing the rooster's alarming crow, he likely felt as though he would never serve Christ again. He was too weak, too wracked with guilt. But the deeply wounded apostle would eventually return to ministerial usefulness on the strength and certainty of Jesus's prayers for him.

Does Jesus pray any less for us? The writer of Hebrews thinks not. "He is able to save to the uttermost those who draw near to God through him, since he always lives to make intercession for them" (Hebrews 7:25). Jesus saves to the uttermost—completely, perfectly[1]—and he never stops praying for those he saves. The trials we encounter only serve to drive us back to Christ and into the sure promises of gospel security in him. That's why Paul could write to the Roman church, in light of assorted trials, "What then shall we say to these things? If God is for us, who can be against us? He who did not spare his own Son but gave him up for us all, how will he not also with him graciously give us all things?" (Romans 8:31–32). Jesus did not exclude pastoral ministry from his promises. He brings pastors into an array of circumstances so that we learn to live life in him. And then we lead our congregations to live likewise.

Begin and Continue in the Gospel

Too many pastors think they can just "do their jobs" and not have many problems. Unfortunately, less than a year of pastoral ministry experience debunks that belief. In my first pastorate, longstanding friction between church members put me in the middle of their barbs. Despite being new to the church, when a decision on selling timber from the church's property arose, I felt the tension. I didn't even know they had timber that could be sold. Of course, one party wanted to sell while the other party thought selling was downright unconscionable. Even in the face of such a trivial decision, I faced a divided congregation. And it was my job to shepherd them to follow Christ. A few years later, I realized that was just a warm-up problem to get me ready for much more. In such circumstances, Jesus calls us to keep living in the gospel.

The gospel is not just a starting point for Christians, it's our whole lives. That's Paul's point to the Colossians: "Therefore, as you received Christ Jesus the Lord, so walk in him, rooted and built up in him and established in the faith, just as you were taught, abounding in thanksgiving" (Colossians 2:6–7). We received Jesus in all his saving power and authority at the start of the Christian life. And now we're called to keep walking in step with him, trusting him as faithful to save *and* sanctify even when things unravel around us. That's how the gospel teaches us to live.

Pastors do not need a different heavenly endowment to serve the church. We need the gospel in the same way as those we shepherd. But here's the problem that creeps into our lives. We can become professional ministers who pontificate on gospel truths while failing to humbly walk in those gospel truths. We spend so much time discussing the gospel that, oddly, we become numb to living in it. Like the plumber whose sink leaks or the investment banker with no savings, pastors can become so busy doing gospel work that we fail to apply the promises of the gospel in daily life. What a shame. What a contradiction.

Raw Edges of Unbelief

Trials in pastoral ministry expose unbelief. Trials grab our attention, and then the dilemma begins. Will we run? Will we lash out in anger and bitterness? Will we lay blame on others? Will we leave the flock we're called to shepherd? Or will we, even through such times, grow in the grace and knowledge of Christ?

As I write, I'm glancing at the biography section in my study. These volumes tell the stories of men whose raw edges were exposed through trials. Polycarp and Ignatius faced Roman execution. Martin Luther dealt with the Zwickau uprising. John Calvin endured conflict with the Genevan council, so much so that he eventually fled. John Bunyan spent more than a dozen years in a Bedford jail because he refused to stop preaching the gospel. Jonathan Edwards was fired from his church despite leading them through two Holy Spirit–led awakenings. Charles Spurgeon faced opposition right and left, from media harassment to unrelenting bodily and emotional trials. Martyn Lloyd-Jones pastored through World War II and preached some Sundays as Axis powers shelled his city with bombs that ultimately scattered his congregation for several years. I could keep going, but the lesson is simple: read about the men who labored before you. Every pastor I've ever read about faced trials, which in turn taught them to rely more and more on Christ.

I remember one particularly difficult period in ministry. Every Sunday, I'd come home exhausted from a busy day and already paralyzed by fears of what might happen the coming week. *Would I be fired? Would I have to take a pay cut?* I developed an unusual Sunday night routine: scouring the help-wanted ads for potential future employment, and reading *The Journals of George Whitefield*. Obviously, the want ads did not edify me! But Whitefield's *Journals* filled me with gospel refreshment. He faced extraordinary opposition during hard times, and the Lord met him over and over. He ended up being an instrument the Lord used to bring many into the kingdom. Over time, I learned to put down the want ads and "stick with Whitefield." In doing so, my spirits lifted, as I turned to the same Christ he trusted to sustain and strengthen me.

Learn to See Trials through a Gospel Lens

I remember Rich calling during the period he describes in this chapter. He had gone through a horrific congregational meeting and felt as though he barely hung on. The remaining church members agonized over the church's plight. Rich unburdened his heart, wondering if he would make it through. I'm sure he thought I was insensitive because I couldn't help but gently laugh. I laughed because I'd walked through similar difficulties. I laughed because he needed to hear the voice of a mentor who loved him reassuring him that his trials were instruments from our loving Father to reshape and reorder his life in more effective service. I laughed because I had shed the same tears and endured the same fears, only to learn of the faithfulness of the one who rose from the dead on our behalf. My gentle laughter offered assurance: Jesus is faithful, trust him. Let me offer a few observations to help pastors who are walking through hard times:

1. Trials will come. The New Testament tells us over and over again: trials will come, and we should never think their presence somehow means the Lord has abandoned us (see Matthew 5:11–12; Luke 9:23–27; 12:11–12; Acts 14:22; Romans 8:18–39; Ephesians 6:12; Philippians 1:29–30; 1 Timothy 1:18–20; 6:3–21; 2 Timothy 3:10–13; 4:1–5). So don't panic. It's normal.

2. Learn to pause in trials instead of rushing into anxiety. When we think our feet have been knocked out from under us, we must work to get our feet on the ground. How? Well, slowly. We read the Word and pray; we meditate on the gospel. If we meditate on the adversity, then we'll only slide deeper into anxiety and fear. So instead, pause to think on Christ. I've turned to Romans 8 more times than I can count. Over and over, the Lord comforts me with his gospel-saturated promises: "For I consider that the sufferings of this present time are not worth comparing with the glory that is to be revealed" (Romans 8:18). I think it takes years to learn to pause instead of immediately reacting. So be patient with yourself.

3. The Lord is more interested in shaping you in his image than in your success. The lure of success blinds many pastors to the beauty of life in Christ. The God who governs the details knows what we need. If his salvific work is for us "to be conformed to the image of his Son" (Romans 8:29), then know that every trial has a gospel-shaped purpose to hone us to think, speak, and act more like our Savior. In other words, perhaps the trial you're facing is God's way of hemming you in, of protecting you from the illusion that you can do anything without his help.

"Live in the gospel." That's not just a nice soundbite to toss around in a sermon. It's the exact reminder you need when trials come.

Young Pastor Rich Applies the Counsel

I understood exactly what Phil meant when he said, "We spend so much time discussing the gospel, that oddly, we become numb to living in it." Even though I had resolved to stay at my church, I was much more *discouraged* about the present situation than I was *encouraged* by the loving embrace of Christ. I had become numb to the promises of God in Christ. Forgiven. Purchased by the blood of Christ. Justified before a holy God. Kept for all eternity in Christ. These beautiful realities were covered by a cloud of despair. They felt distant, as if they were meant for someone else. You may be at a low point in ministry right now. You've labored with all your might, and all you can see is defeat. If this describes you, let me encourage not to give up. Keep looking to Jesus.

Imagine you're stranded in your car on a cold winter night. As you walk to find help, you notice a faint glow in the distance. When you draw closer, it's apparent that you're approaching a fire. Now, pause and think about this picture. What's the logical next step? Clearly, it makes sense to get warm by the fire. It would be unthinkable to stand off at a distance, just close enough to observe the fire, but far enough to remain cold.

Sadly, sometimes we get close enough to the Word to observe who Christ is and point others to him. Yet we stay far enough away that we fail to experience the joy of our Savior. Christ wants his undershepherds to draw close to him, delight in him, and learn from him. *Only then* can we shepherd God's people to enjoy Christ.

Remember: pastors are sheep first, then shepherds. Should we not also enjoy the Savior we preach? We pray you'll find joy in the Savior, whatever the trial. In his little book *Looking unto Jesus*, Theodore Monod records his meditation on those three words found in Hebrews 12:2. "Looking unto Jesus and not at what we are doing for Him. Too much occupied with our work, we can forget our Master,—it is possible to have hands full and heart empty. When occupied with our Master, we cannot forget our work; if the heart is filled with His love, how can the hands fail to be active in His service?"[2]

 ## Mentor Phil Lists Some Next Steps

- As you face adversities, do a fresh reading of the Gospels. Look at your Lord Jesus. See how he endured suffering. Take notes on how Jesus depended upon the Father, gave thanks instead of complained, and served others even when opposed. Go back over your notes and then consider how you might emulate Christ in your life.
- After you have read the Gospels and taken notes on what you learn about Jesus's dependence on the

Father, begin to read through the Epistles. Notice how Christocentric they are. Jot down the various ways the authors apply the gospel to broad issues of life. Then again review your notes to see how you might better apply the gospel in ways the Epistles teach.

- Read the Puritans who lived constantly in adversity and understood what it meant to live in Christ. Be helped by their wisdom and ability to apply the gospel to all life's challenges. A few Puritan titles that might encourage you are *The Bruised Reed* by Richard Sibbes, *The Rare Jewel of Christian Contentment* by Jeremiah Burroughs, *Precious Remedies Against Satan's Devices* by Thomas Brooks, and *The Glory of Christ* by John Owen (all are Banner of Truth Puritan Paperbacks). If you're not accustomed to reading the Puritans, you might find that reading them aloud, at first, will help you to get the most out of their richness. Read them with a pencil in hand to underline citations you want to remember. Be sure to pause and meditate and pray on particularly helpful lines.

- Intensify your prayer life. Pray more than "please get me out of this jam." Pray to know the Lord through suffering (see examples in 2 Corinthians 4:16–18 and Philippians 3:10–11). Prayer becomes the means to move attention away from self and onto Christ and his sufficiency.

- Keep your mind steady on pastoral ministry. It's easy to slide into self-pity or self-focus due to the adversities about you. But you've been called to shepherd the flock. Concentrate, by God's grace, on feeding the congregation the Word. Pray for your members. Speak comfort and encouragement to those who need comfort and encouragement; offer direction to those who need direction. You may find that focusing on others frees you from inward contemplation.

Recommended Reading

Safe and Sound: Standing Firm in Spiritual Battles by David Powlison

Deserted by God? Understanding the Ways of God through the Experience of the Psalmists by Sinclair Ferguson

Part 4
The Fruitful Years

And let us not grow weary of doing good,
for in due season we will reap, if we do not give up.
So then, as we have opportunity, let us do good
to everyone, and especially to those who are
of the household of faith.

Galatians 6:9–10

8.

Layer Teaching to Make Changes

 Young Pastor Rich Faces a Challenge

I've heard it said that it takes seven years to really become the pastor of a church. That seems anecdotally true. To get to know a congregation, gain trust, lay a solid doctrinal foundation, and lead through significant changes usually doesn't happen quickly. It takes time and patience to earn a congregation's trust. You laugh and cry together; you forgive each other and rejoice with one another; you encourage and exhort each other; you experience the complexities of church life together. It's normal. It's the way God designed it as he brings redeemed sinners together to learn to live as followers of Jesus.

Put another way, pastoral ministry rarely offers a straightforward path from reality to biblical aspirations. It's more like navigating a maze. Sometimes you make a wrong turn and have to redirect. Throughout the process, you continue to seek the Lord through his Word, prayer, and godly counsel. And eventually, you've built up enough trust for the congregation to follow your leadership.

Significant Changes

Churches must ask the question, where are we? How did we get here? Perhaps, like the church at Sardis in Revelation 3:1–6, a church once had the reputation of being alive but now it stands on the cusp of death. So, what happened? Evaluating the root of decline may clarify the path toward revitalization.

Audubon Park was like Sardis. We had a reputation of being alive *in the past*. But over time we had slowly declined. And if change were to happen, I knew I must lead. I saw areas needing change but wasn't sure how to get there. I had gained the church's trust but had no clue what to do next.

Let me explain a few of our most obvious problems.

Church Membership

The membership roll at Audubon Park was, well, bloated. Our roll listed more than a thousand members, but on Sunday morning, we'd be glad to crest one hundred. Paul describes the church as a body in 1 Corinthians 12:12. How can a member claim to be joined to the body of Christ when always absent? This glaring discrepancy raised a few questions: Did the church think having 90 percent of members *in absentia* followed Scripture? Did our bylaws offer counsel for solving this dilemma? Did anyone know anything about what our bylaws said? Did previous pastors teach on regenerate membership, which happens to be a historically distinguishing mark of our denomination?

Over my first six years, we removed a few members, primarily because we discovered they were deceased. We slowly did some work to locate other members and continued to clean up the rolls. But we needed to do more than that. We needed to totally reframe the church's concept of membership by starting with basic questions: Who can join the church? Is church membership even biblical? If so, what are the requirements for membership? Does a potential new member need to be acquainted with the history of the church? What does the church believe, and does the prospective member have to agree with the church's doctrinal statement? What is expected of members that isn't expected of non-members? I taught on the subject when it came up in preaching texts but hadn't made any real effort to change our membership process. How would we make real change?

The Church's Mission and Ministries

Audubon Park had a great history of supporting missionaries and making disciples locally. Church records indicate significant financial support to global missions and ministries within the church that helped members grow in Christ. But the "going" aspect of missions had faded. We gave to international missions annually but lacked other supported workers. We certainly encouraged our members to give to missions, but at the same time, we couldn't maintain a balanced budget. Changes needed to be made that would allow us to steward our resources well, which included giving to missions.

Simply put, we couldn't maintain our existing trellises. In fact, even trying to maintain those structures was making it difficult to do more worthwhile work. So, what could we do? How could we get back to the basics of the church's mission of making disciples and teaching them how to grow in maturity?

How Do Significant Changes Happen?

I remember talking with Phil about this season of ministry. It looked like the church was going to survive and I would remain as pastor. Slowly, we started seeing new growth. Remaining members and newer members started to form relationships. God began raising up a little sapling that needed direction, instruction, and leadership. The church trusted me and I sensed we could handle more significant change. Previously, I'd asked myself, "How do I hang on?" *But now* the question had shifted: "How do I lead?"

Phil's counsel shaped the way we sought to implement change into the life of the church. Essentially, here's what he said, "Keep doing what you're doing, but press into it." Or: *Layer teaching with more teaching* from God's Word before you make any changes.

 Mentor Phil Offers Counsel

Every church faces change. Congregations morph in different ways over the years. The church's grasp of its mission and ministry grows or declines. A new pastor with a different ministry bent and experience arrives and shakes things up.

With change usually comes discomfort. Only a thoughtless pastor demands change with little concern about how it brings upheaval to expectations and rhythms in life and ministry. Pastoral leadership must welcome the uncomfortable practice of change if such changes will more closely align a congregation to God's Word. However, even justifiable changes must be paired with patience and wisdom. Healthy change leads to healthy churches. But healthy change requires a Christ-honoring process.

Changes by Leadership, Not Decree

Authoritarian pastors decree changes unilaterally. What they say goes. When they decide a change must happen, they order it, accepting nothing less than wholesale cooperation. This approach stifles grace-filled Christianity and has no place in the local church.

Consider instead the New Testament pattern for pastors. Peter's description of shepherding the flock calls for leading changes through godly example, "not lording it over those entrusted to you" (1 Peter 5:3 NIV). The writer of Hebrews instructs the church to submit to its leaders as those leaders exercise care for them, knowing they will give an account to the Lord of the church (13:17). Indeed, pastors must lead. They should even expect their flock to follow. Yet they do so with the desire to care for the congregation's spiritual lives and the certainty that they will give an account for everything to the Lord Jesus.

Effective leadership toward change requires wisdom. It requires pastors to know their church and to know their Bibles. For example, if you're the new pastor of a church that hasn't practiced meaningful membership in decades, then you know that implementing church discipline eventually needs to happen. But first, such a church needs to understand the gospel and repentance and what a local church is. Only after that foundation has been laid can you even begin to try and explain to them what the Bible says about church polity. Wise leaders will pump the brakes before making a change that will be misunderstood. First things first.

Layer Change

Those who have been around me for long know that I love the word *layer* when I'm talking about making changes in ministry. Layering means we don't announce a change—for example, meaningful membership—simply by declaring it. We emphasize teaching the foundational truths so that God's Word remains at the forefront. This teaching will happen in different venues: Sunday morning sermon, Sunday school, mid-week small groups, or book studies. I appreciate small groups because they allow for discussion. Good discussion allows for the congregation to dialogue about the *truth* as they seek to understand any proposed changes. Layering helps us avoid misunderstandings. It also forces us to slow down. If a church has a high regard for the Word, then patient teaching on a biblical practice—even one that's been rejected—will generally persuade those willing to be persuaded.

Too many pastors want things to change too quickly. Too many pastors want their congregations to effortlessly embrace truths we've taken years to appreciate and understand. But that's impossible, even for the most effective teachers. And brothers, I promise you're not that effective either!

The church is a conglomeration of young and old, mature and immature, well-read and poorly read, good listeners and poor listeners, people eager for growth and people skeptical of growth. Those who listen well and exhibit maturity will generally embrace change more readily. But what percentage of the church fits that bill? Maybe a lot, maybe just a few. We cannot just focus on the mature. Shepherding the flock requires shepherding *all the flock,* even the stragglers who seem resistant to biblical truth. So we must remain patient—through our teaching, our small-group discussions, our conversations over coffee, and every interaction we have. All of it is an aspect of the church's ongoing discipleship.

Layering, Modeling, and Praying

Let's get practical for a second. Once you determine which changes need to be made, you then need to teach on the subject from various angles and various venues. Make sure you're regularly inviting and answering questions with respect and kindness. If some act huffy over what you're teaching, that's fine. Listen to them. Ask them questions. Never treat them like misbehaving children. Love them with the truth of the Word. As you lead with grace, your church members will more likely listen.

When the apostles told the early church in Acts 6:4 that they would give themselves to prayer and the ministry of the word, they meant *both*. And so we too must pray for the effectiveness of the spoken word. We must pray for teachable hearts. We must pray for humility to speak and to listen. We must pray for renewed minds that intend to obey Christ. Finally, we must pray for any spiritual strongholds to be broken and brought into captivity to Christ.

Let me give you an example of how this played out in our church. Our elders wanted to lead us to engage an unreached people group for the first time. We knew this decision would both limit and expand how we engaged in missions. So we layered the change.

First, we hosted a missionary from the region. He spoke several times to our congregation and even endured a few challenging question-and-answer sessions. We sent several short-term teams to visit the people group, and had our members report back to the congregation upon their return. We provided a steady stream of information about the people group, often praying for workers among them in our worship gatherings.

This process made the change happen slowly but without much difficulty. Previously, our missions money had primarily funded construction projects in areas already saturated with Christians. Now we funded evangelism and missionary support among unreached people.

 ## Young Pastor Rich Applies the Counsel

The most significant lesson I learned during this season of ministry is the importance of repetition. Or, as Paul says to Timothy, preach the Word "with complete patience and teaching" (2 Timothy 4:2). Patience coupled with teaching implies repetition.

What Phil said above is so true: too many pastors want their congregations to effortlessly embrace truths we've taken years to appreciate and understand. That's so convicting, but I'm not sure I learned it until several years into ministry. A decade in, I've genuinely come to enjoy the process of layering the truth of God's Word into the minds and hearts of his people. I find much joy in seeing the lights come on. It's so much more satisfying, and so much more humbling, to see God's Word do the work. "Here's what I think we should do—just trust me" may sound like leadership. But it's far from it.

After Change

When the change is made, it's tempting to think the work is done. But not so fast! We need to layer teaching even *after* change. For example, in my early days at Audubon Park, anyone could join the church on any given Sunday. A person could come forward after the sermon, express a desire to join, share a conversion testimony, and the congregation would vote to receive that person as a member.

After seven years, we changed the membership process. Honestly, at that point I thought—or at least I hoped—that my work was done. But I didn't realize that I needed to *keep teaching* on the importance of meaningful church membership. Church membership means much more than how to receive members. Suddenly, we had important questions to answer: What happens when a member doesn't gather with the church body for an extended period of time? What kind of responsibility do church members have toward those who neglect fellowship with other believers?

As we began to clean up our membership rolls, I found a surprising reality: some folks wanted to remain a member but not be involved in the life of the church in any way. No, I'm not talking about homebound saints. I'm talking about perfectly healthy folks who simply refused to come to church but wanted to stay on the roll. I tried to teach our church that these folks should be removed. Some of our members balked. This situation provided an opportunity to layer more teaching on church membership and encourage member-on-member care. How can a foot or hand or eye or ear be a part of the body if it isn't joined with it, as explained in 1 Corinthians 12? How can a member grow in grace with other members when he or she is never there?

Pastors, slow down and enjoy the process of layering. As you teach, trust in the ordinary means of grace. Certainly, God equips his undershepherds with skills that are useful for the good of his churches. But don't let your persuasive abilities, your savvy people skills, or your confident ingenuity bypass God's design. Instead, be patient, trust the Word, layer teaching with more teaching, and watch God work.

Mentor Phil Lists Some Next Steps

- Identify any areas of church life and ministry that run contrary to Scripture. Prioritize what might be changed quickly (for example, preaching expositionally instead of topically) to what needs layering to achieve (changing the church's leadership structure).

- Be careful not to allow areas of change to run ahead of laying a strong gospel foundation. Teach your people to listen and respond to the Word. Don't sacrifice weekly exposition out of eagerness to change something that bothers you.

- Project what it will take to establish major changes, such as leadership changes or covenant membership. How can you layer teaching on these areas? Who are the influencers in the church that you might disciple? Would it be useful or polarizing to bring in someone to speak on these issues? Are there some written materials you can distribute among the congregation to help layer change?

- Decide when the congregation appears ready for a particular change. Bathe your approach in prayer. Be a good listener. Stay focused on the teaching of Scripture. Lead with patience and humility. Establish the necessary changes without castigating those before who either failed to give attention to Scripture or did not realize that tradition had become an idol.

Recommended Reading

The 9Marks book *Character Matters: Shepherding in the Fruit of the Spirit* by Aaron Menikoff

Finding the Right Hills to Die On: The Case for Theological Triage by Gavin Ortlund

The 9Marks book *The Compelling Community: Where God's Power Makes a Church Attractive* by Mark Dever and Jamie Dunlop

The 9Marks Church Questions series of short books

Church Membership: How the World Knows Who Represents Jesus by Jonathan Leeman in the 9Marks Building Healthy Churches collection

9.

Lead the Church to Biblical Polity

 Young Pastor Rich Faces a Challenge

The title of this chapter may entice you to keep reading, *or* to move on to the next. Not every church needs to change its leadership structure. Some churches have already established the importance of elder plurality. But in many instances, new pastors face an unhealthy leadership structure. Often, churches give too much authority to one man. The New Testament opposes this practice. When Paul called for the leaders of the church at Ephesus to meet with him, he called for the *elders* of the church. He didn't single out any one particular pastor (Acts 20). The same with Peter when he exhorted the elders to shepherd the flock (1 Peter 5). The New Testament uses the terms *elder*, *overseer*, and *pastor* interchangeably to describe one office.

In God's wisdom he has ordered the church to be led by a plurality of elders. There are obvious benefits to local churches for having a plurality of pastors rather than a single pastor. Accountability among leadership, more eyes and ears to protect the church from false teaching, more voices to teach correct doctrine, and more availability for pastoral care, just to name a few. But our church didn't have this structure in place.

I knew we had to move in this direction if the church would sustain biblical vitality in the long run.

As I write this chapter, I'm looking at a pictureless frame sitting on my desk. Sound strange? Well, there's something inside the frame: a ballot. At the top it reads, "Pastor Vote: March 18, 2018." The ballot is from the day the church voted to install a plurality of elders. It was a historical moment in the life of the church. Since its start in 1944, the church only had experience with single-pastor polity. On this ballot are three potential elders, with a yes or no next to each name.

On this particular ballot, the one I framed, each received a checkmark—three checkmarks signifying a unanimous no. Why did I frame such discouragement? Because this no-vote ballot reminds me of God's kindness. After all, it's the *only* ballot checked with any nos. After much study on the importance of elder plurality, virtually the entire church agreed that it was time to move in this direction.

Biblical leadership—and the polity that supports it—is one of the most important indications of healthy church life. I know, I know. It sounds like a cliché: everything rises and falls on leadership. Peter exhorts the *elders* in 1 Peter 5:2 to "shepherd the flock of God that is among you." God ordained a pattern of leadership for his church. Sheep need shepherds. So how does a pastor who has earned the trust of a congregation lead in changing a church's polity?

You may remember Phil's counsel in the previous chapter: keep doing what you're doing, but press in with more intensity. I tried to put that advice into practice. If the text I preached raised the question of church leadership, I would address it. I remember preaching through the book of Philippians and immediately tackling the issue of church leadership because the very first verse addressed it: "To all the saints in Christ Jesus who are at Philippi, with the overseers and deacons" (Philippians 1:1). This was the first book I preached through at Audubon Park. I began the layering process by identifying the distinction in these two offices.

I tried to do the same in my personal relationships. If a church member and I were having a conversation and the topic of church leadership came up, I would lean in instead of dodge the topic. I remember several conversations about what it meant to have a senior pastor and other "staff ministers" who weren't understood to be co-equals alongside me. I would explain how our current model did not reflect the New Testament's teaching on elders. Sometimes, these comments were met with warmth. Other times, they were met with suspicion. But after years of shepherding, I gained the church's trust. And it eventually seemed like the right time to press into this area with more focus.

But what conditions made this new opportunity apparent?

Trust Was Built

Back in seminary, when I first began to desire the work of church revitalization, I remember reading Mark Dever and Paul Alexander's book *Deliberate Church*. It captivated me, particularly their explanation of the four Ps of pastoral ministry: preaching, praying, personal discipleship, and patience.[1]

I took the four Ps as simple but profound biblical counsel. In a time where pragmatism ruled the day, they refreshed me. I wanted to see God take a church from death to life through his Word and his Spirit.

In my first ten years at Audubon Park, I made *plenty* of mistakes. Plenty! My weaknesses, faults, and shortcomings were readily available for all to see. But by God's grace, I did my best to pastor with these four Ps in mind. Eventually, the church recognized my desire to lead toward biblical reform. Perhaps most significantly, they realized that my intentions were for their good and God's glory. I had no hidden agenda or desire to use the church as a rung up the ministry ladder. I only desired to faithfully pastor the flock entrusted to my care.

Illusions Dissipated

During this period, it also began to register with the congregation that one man can't shepherd a flock alone. If he could, Scripture's emphasis on plurality (seen in passages like Acts 14:23 and Titus 1:5) would be amiss. While other paradigms of shared leadership may help curtail the weaknesses of a single pastor, churches need collective pastoral care.

I learned so much from the pastors who mentored me at South Woods before I set out. I watched as the elders shepherded their flock together. I heard them pray for suffering saints. I listened to them discuss vision and mission for the church, and work toward unity, even when it was difficult. I observed with intrigue how they handled disagreements, and I received deep encouragement watching their brotherly love toward one another. Simply put, in addition to the biblical witness, the elders at South Woods convinced me that a plurality of elders was a gift to the church.

Even in my early years that followed at Audubon Park, I still took time to invest in men whom I thought might serve the church one day as elders. I didn't know when or if the day would come, but I wanted to make sure to prepare certain men for the task. I read good books with these men on church leadership, such as *Nine Marks of a Healthy Church* by Mark

Dever, *The Shepherd Leader* by Timothy Witmer, and Phil's book *Elders in Congregational Life.*

But the most effective strategy that fostered the right conditions for change was not anything I did, but the fact that certain men were already doing the work of an elder. And they weren't doing it because I told them to or suggested it! In fact, it was quite the opposite. These men just shepherded the saints because *they were shepherds.* They were unofficial elders caring for the flock. And the church took notice, which set the stage for our overwhelmingly positive vote for plural leadership polity.

How to Lead the Church to Change

As I cultivated trust, our church lost the illusion that a single pastor was enough, and a group of unofficial elders set a positive example. These three things prepared us for elder plurality. But we weren't there yet. Though the seeds had been planted, there was still work left to do.

Of course, it was Phil who helped me remember this. I encourage you to observe his counsel.

 Mentor Phil Offers Counsel

I made the mistake of not clearly establishing biblical polity when I planted the church I serve. I jokingly told a few people, "The church's polity is between my ears." That put us in a tenuous position. On one hand, I could easily make up polity decisions as I went along. While I would hope to have followed Scripture, that might not have happened. Without a guiding polity document shaped by God's Word, we could have easily slipped into unhealthy patterns. On the other hand, if something had suddenly happened to me, even the polity "between my ears" would vanish, leaving the church without a scrap of organization.

Thankfully, as I studied the Word, I came to strong convictions on biblical church polity. I ended up putting into practice these nine facets for establishing polity change. **1. Model pastoral care.** Pastors care for the flock. Regardless of how elaborate the structure or how qualified the elders may be, without attention to the flock it will not matter. If you want to change polity to reflect biblical shepherding, then you must shepherd the flock. Give attention, as best you can, to teaching, training, comforting, encouraging, correcting, and caring for those under your care. Your model as a pastor will encourage future elders as they join you.

2. Emphasize organic relationships. Instead of putting all the promotion and focus on programs and structures, emphasize relationships. Enlarge the church's vision for living life together in Christ, serving one another, and visibly displaying the gospel through relationships.[2] Particularly in church revitalizations, church members need to be taught not to equate church life with particular programs and traditions. So spend time through sermons, Bible studies, applications, illustrations, and communication to help them understand that personal relationships matter.

3. Encourage members to serve one another. I remember my first study on the New Testament *one another* passages. It changed the way that I, as a solo pastor, saw the church. I realized that so much of my thinking, which obviously spilled over into pastoral work and preaching, centered on structures instead of on one another. Until church members see the priority of serving one another, then the church remains stiff and stagnant. Through preaching and teaching, raise the congregation's expectations of how they ought to relate to one another. As church members learn to serve one other, the church more clearly lives out its identity as the blood-bought people of God. What does this have to do with polity? A congregation grasping the massive challenge of the *one another* passages will recognize the need for help—lots of help—to understand what that looks like. A plurality of elders leads the way. They teach, train, encourage, and model Christian service.

4. Layer teaching on polity. Rich mentioned preaching through Philippians in the early stage of his revitalization work at Audubon Park. Look for other passages in the normal course of exposition by which you can layer polity. Does the text raise questions about decision-making, qualities for leaders, the church's gatherings, discipline, or another issue that needs the work of elders? Let biblical theology go to work. How does the church at large deal with an issue the size of the one in 1 Corinthians 5, where a scandalously immoral man needed firm discipline, without plural elder involvement? Or how does the church appropriately address the legalistic teaching that crept into the Galatian churches without a plurality of elders examining, exposing, and correcting those involved? Who are the pastors and teachers that equip the saints and build up the body of Christ in Ephesians 4? Whether working through an expositional series or teaching in a Bible class or leading a devotional prayer time or reading a book together, layer the Bible's teaching on church polity.

5. Discuss and study polity with the current leadership structure, whatever that structure may be. In our church's process toward biblical polity, leading the *de facto* leaders through a study of what the Bible had to say about leadership, church offices, and church structure moved us ahead toward embracing biblical polity. It was not a quick study. We took about fifteen months (meeting once or twice a month) to work through every passage in the Bible that had something to do with these issues. I had Bible dictionaries, concordances (yes, that was the old days), word studies, and commentaries available, as we sat around a table and discussed God's Word. We made the study Word-centered rather than reading a book on polity (few existed then). Once we made our way through the Scripture, we put together a short document on our findings to share with the congregation. We concluded, without qualms, that biblical church polity required elder plurality to shepherd the church and deacon plurality to serve the church. Today, there are many excellent books on biblical polity that can help, including those listed at the end of this chapter.

6. Highlight the character requirements for church leaders. Aside from "apt to teach," the qualifications for elders could be described as *just be model Christians*. Elders must be temperate and self-controlled. They must be hospitable. They must be faithful husbands and fathers who have a good reputation among outsiders. All of that should be normal for every follower of Christ. The 1 Timothy 3 and Titus 1 characteristics help the church to see what mature Christianity looks like. Over time, as you teach passages like 1 Peter 5, the church will begin to understand this. Polity is just a tool—a good one. But unless those discharging it walk with Christ, polity will not accomplish what it's intended to do.

7. Broaden circles from the earlier study with church leaders. The goal in studying polity is ultimately to reach the church at large. A good way to start is to begin with a few key leaders, taking as long as necessary to work through the Scriptures together. Then move to a wider circle, like deacons or a leadership board. Again, take whatever time is necessary within your church's present structure to let them see what God's Word teaches.[3] Keep widening the circles of study and discussion until you're able to bring the entire study to the congregation.

8. Intentionally teach through the Pastoral Epistles. What better place to see biblical polity unpacked than in the Pastoral Epistles? In these books, church life is front and center. The qualifications and job descriptions for elders and deacons couldn't be clearer. Each of these epistles also deals with areas of pastoral instruction and correction. Let Scripture do the work. Just expound and apply it. I also suggest adding some opportunities for discussion on the expositions along the way, just so members have a chance to ask questions and get clarification on unfamiliar concepts.

9. Present, discuss, vote, examine, approve, and install new elders. This process will likely take years. For Rich, it took six to seven years before his congregation appeared ready to approve the changes. He wisely did not rush toward polity change. The goal isn't to disrupt the church but to bring them along to trust the revelation of God's Word. You'll also need to formally rework any existing polity documents, like a church constitution or bylaws. You can then present these changes to the church so they can ask questions and ultimately vote to pass something they've seen and understand. The day to vote on the changes will be an important step in the church's life. Once the church approves a new governing structure, then comes the vital work of nominating qualified men to serve as elders. Once the church has some time to examine and affirm those men, then the church can celebrate with an installation service.

You may add or subtract from my nine facets, but whatever you decide, develop a process by which you can patiently, biblically train the congregation in New Testament church polity. I've often been asked how long the start-to-finish process takes. That varies with each church. Most importantly, love your church through the process of letting go of long-held ideas. Whether it takes two or five or eight years, cherish every moment. You're teaching your people what Christ has given for his church to mature. That spiritual work requires spiritual men serving the body in a spiritual way.

 ## Young Pastor Rich Applies the Counsel

The time was right. Our current leadership was on board with changing our polity. As the time grew closer for change, we studied polity in smaller settings like classes and small groups. I remember one occasion when a polity light bulb began to glow. We were going through a book study on Sunday evenings, *What Is a Healthy Church?* by Mark Dever. Church members were reading the assigned chapters in advance, and then I would teach from that chapter. The last chapter was on biblical church leadership. That evening, I clearly remember explaining from Acts 20 verses 17 and 28 how Luke uses three words to describe the office of elder. Two are nouns: *elder* and *overseer*. The third is a verb: *to shepherd* or *to care for*. But as a noun it is translated "shepherd" or "pastor" (as in Ephesians 4:11). In that moment, the church began viewing the term *elder* in a positive light. I recall one person who had always endorsed a single-pastor model verbally acknowledging that elders, overseers, and pastors are all the same. I smiled, nodded, and said yes as my heart leaped with joy! The Word of God flipped the switch.

With all these factors in place, I began talking with our deacons about rewriting the constitution and bylaws to better reflect our beliefs and processes for certain things. We needed to decide how we would select new elders, how we would take in members, how we would practice church discipline, how we would use our church covenant, and how we would decide who decides what. We worked through that process for about six months. Then, when the new constitution was written, we went through a review process with the congregation for another three to four months. Once the constitution was approved by the congregation, we began the process of selecting our first team of elders. As I think about Phil's counsel above, there are two points of encouragement I want to share with you that sound contradictory: Don't rush. Don't delay.

1. Don't rush. Of the nine practices Phil mentioned, all have at least one common denominator. *Time.* If a church's polity is going to change, a pastor cannot rush the process. For instance, before the church selected our current elders, it was clear to me that they should be elders. But it was important for the church to see this. And they did, with time. Part of the process that narrowed the focus on changing our polity involved giving these men more regular opportunities to teach and serve the congregation as elders would. This helped raise the congregation's awareness of these men who were already functioning as elders in certain ways. The church observed their character and enjoyed their giftedness. Eventually, when the moment arrived to ask the church for nominations, it was clear whom God had raised up among us.

2. Don't delay. The process also shouldn't be delayed. Dragging a process out can stifle a church's morale. A fruit that hangs on a tree will eventually rot if not picked. Once it was apparent that the church was ready to move in this direction, *I kept the process going.* I preached a sermon series on the offices in the local church. I asked questions of the biblical text like, "Who leads the church? What's the difference between elders and deacons? Why does this matter?" Once I finished the series, we moved into a time of nominating, vetting, training, and affirming these men as elders. It was an exciting time in the life of Audubon Park. Was it a perfect process? No. Did we have challenges along the way? Of course! But at some point, to see biblical change in polity, you must *move* toward change.

 Mentor Phil Lists Some Next Steps

- Evaluate your present church polity in light of Scripture's teaching. Consider what needs to be changed to be consistent with Scripture.
- After adequate time to gain the congregation's trust, take the main leaders of the church through a biblical study of polity. Let them be involved in reading, researching, and recording conclusions.
- Put together a document detailing New Testament church polity. Decide what changes need to take place in the current church governing documents to come in line with Scripture.
- Work out from the leadership group to broader circles, teaching on what you've concluded.

- Patiently teach the whole church. Give them time to absorb, ask questions, study Scripture, and prepare for changes.
- Implement the changes to the church's governing documents. Let the church vote on the changes.
- Pray for the Lord to raise up godly, qualified men to serve as elders. Develop a process for selection, training, and installation.

Recommended Reading

The 9Marks book *Elders in the Life of the Church: Rediscovering the Biblical Model for Church Leadership* by Phil A. Newton and Matt Schmucker

Church Elders: How to Shepherd God's People Like Jesus by Jeramie Rinne in the 9Marks Building Healthy Churches collection

The 9Marks book *Finding Faithful Elders and Deacons* by Thabiti M. Anyabwile

Deacons: How They Serve and Strengthen the Church by Matt Smethurst in the 9Marks Building Healthy Churches collection

The 9Marks book *Word-Centered Church: How the Scripture Brings Life and Growth to God's People* by Jonathan Leeman

10.

Build a Culture of Discipleship

 **Young Pastor Rich Faces a Challenge**

The three elders—Dallas, Don, and I—sat around a conference table praying. We asked God for wisdom to lead the church God had entrusted to our care. The joyful but sobering reality settled into us: the church had elected its first set of elders. Whatever happened next was new for us and the church. Thankfully, the elders at South Woods and Grace Church (another sister church) welcomed us to sit in on elders' meetings to observe. Furthermore, we all read and discussed good books on elder plurality, like those recommended in the previous chapter. But at some point, we knew we'd have to get rid of the training wheels and sit on the bike and ride. The road ahead would be a path of learning. So we retreated to spend time praying, planning, and thanking God for the changes that had happened at Audubon Park. Out of that elders' retreat came three areas of focus: (1) leading in unity, (2) building a culture of discipleship, and (3) training leaders.

Leading in Unity

Now that we had embraced this change, we faced new questions. How do we lead together? As we lead together in unity, where do we focus our attention? With biblical polity in place, and a desire to let the Word of God lead us, we aimed at getting back to the basics taught and modeled by Jesus and his apostles. We knew that Christ's mission remained the same for all churches. So, we spent time discussing and clarifying why our church, or any church for that matter, exists.

Building a Culture of Discipleship

The mission of the church is spelled out clearly in Matthew 28:18–20. Jesus tells his disciples, "All authority in heaven and on earth has been given to me. Go therefore and make disciples of all nations, baptizing them in the name of the Father and of the Son and of the Holy Spirit, teaching them to observe all that I have commanded you. And behold, I am with you always, to the end of the age." While Jesus initially gave this Great Commission to the apostles, the book of Acts offers ample examples of how the apostles entrusted the commission to local churches and the elders that served them (see Acts 14:21–23; 16:1–5; 20:17–32). We knew coming out of our retreat that building a culture of discipleship was the mission we wanted to communicate to the church. It wasn't something new, but it had gotten lost in the trellises. And we were all on board. Together we concluded from our study of the Scriptures and time in prayer that the church exists to worship God and to bring others into fellowship with him by making his Son known. How would we as elders of the church equip our members to make disciples of Jesus?

One question arises when thinking about elders leading in unity to carry out a biblical vision of disciple-making. To what extent should nonpaid elders engage in building a culture of discipleship? Let me explain. When a church is accustomed to paying a solo pastor to do "the work of ministry"—a misunderstanding of Ephesians 4:12—it's assumed that he will be responsible for a majority of the teaching (particularly in corporate gatherings), evangelism, and oversight of all the ministries of the church. But elder plurality signals a shift toward *shared leadership*. As elders equip the church together, disciple-making becomes a key area of shared leadership. So how does an elder team work together to build a culture of discipleship? What is expected of an elder's time when he works a full-time job outside of the church? Will nonpaid elders be responsible for teaching, organizing ministries, and one-on-one discipleship?

Training Leaders

The disciple-making process includes training future leaders for the church. Paul's words to Timothy ring clearly: "If anyone aspires to the office of overseer, he desires a noble task" (1 Timothy 3:1). A church should ask, "How will any man aspire to the office if discipleship for pastoral ministry doesn't exist?"

Once a church establishes elders, it could be easy to assume that the work of training elders just evolves naturally. But what happens when a church grows and needs more shepherds? Or, what if an elder needs to step away for a season? Are there enough elders to bear the extra load of soul care? What if churches needing pastors call for help in recommending a pastor? Would you have any men in your congregation to recommend? What if you recognize an underserved area locally or globally that needs a new church? Could you send a pastor, a missionary, or a team? These are all important questions that affirm the need to build a culture of discipleship in the life of a local church. It recognizes that we do not exist on an island as a local church, but we're part of a global expression of Christ's body.

How Do We Disciple to Raise Up Future Elders?

How do elders lead a church to be able to meet these kinds of kingdom needs? Once again, Phil's counsel has shaped our approach. The counsel here doesn't begin only when biblical polity is in place. Instead, building a culture of discipleship encompasses the entire process described in this book. It begins on day one of the new pastorate.

But maybe you find yourself thanking God for raising up other godly elders to shepherd the flock with you. Maybe church membership has much more meaning than it once did. Maybe you have the church's trust. Maybe your focus is now more centered on the mission of the church because God has granted health to the congregation. Let me encourage you, consider the counsel that follows.

If you've been pastoring for long, you've probably already discovered an unfortunate reality in pastoral ministry: it's tempting to make the mission of the church something other than what Christ tells us it is. We live in a time when many voices are telling the church to focus on fill-in-the-blank. But pastors, the mission of the church is to make disciples of Jesus Christ. Pastoral ministry prepares disciples for the coming new creation Jesus promised. Work hard at building a culture of discipleship.

Mentor Phil Offers Counsel

When Jesus said, "Follow me," he called people to be disciples. In its simplest form, to be a disciple means to be a learner. As Mark Dever put it, "To be a Christian means to be a disciple. There are no Christians who are not disciples."[1] In other words, members of Christ's church are disciples, those who follow Jesus and learn from him. Disciple-making is the path to healthy congregationalism. It can't be merely a tangential part of the church's ministry. It's central—or at least it should be.

The Problem of Superficial Activities

Somewhere along the way, I began to believe the lie that a busy calendar equated to a healthy church. I believed this until I got married and realized I had wounded my new bride. As a single man, I had time on my hands to invest in the church where I served. And I used it daily. Because of this, I got into some patterns that left me with virtually no time after marriage to spend with my wife. I taught Sunday school, I preached, I taught on Sunday afternoon, I led a youth discipleship group on Monday night, I led a young adult discipleship group on Tuesday night, I taught the youth group on Wednesday night, I participated in visitation on Thursday night, and I tagged on for a youth activity on either Friday or Saturday night. Then the process started all over the next week.

I was in my last year of college, while my wife commuted thirty minutes early each weekday to her job. Our schedules precluded quality time together. Three months after saying I do, I came into our living room to find her in the middle of the floor crying. I wondered what in the world bothered her. Turns out, it was me. I had so overscheduled my life that I neglected to shepherd her. I had neglected managing my own household well and faced the stinging indictment: "If a man does not know how to manage his own household, how will he take care of the church of God?" (1 Timothy 3:5 NASB). I began to reorder my priorities and life, realizing that we can become immersed in doing lots of good things while failing at the most basic level of Christian discipleship—in the home.

In some sense, my experience serves as a parable for much of the evangelical church world. Stay busy, plan lots of activities, do lots of good things, keep the calendar full, and you will be spiritually healthy. But is that spiritual health? I don't think so. Spiritual health is about a relationship with the Lord that manifests itself in relationship with others. Jesus told Peter, "Simon, son of John, do you love Me more than these?" A bit perturbed, Peter let Jesus know he did love him. Then the Lord told him what this love looks like: "Tend My lambs." The question followed twice, with similar responses by Jesus, "Shepherd My sheep. . . . Tend My sheep" (John 21:15–17 NASB).

Does this imply that everything we do must be in an auditorium or classroom or small group with Bibles and notebooks out? I'd suggest not, since the relational nature of disciple-making means we'll spend a lot of time just being with one another. Günter Krallmann calls it with-ness, or the "dynamic process of life-transference" that Jesus modeled with the Twelve.[2] When Jesus called the Twelve, Mark narrates that he called them to be "with him" (Mark 3:14). They laughed, discussed, debated, teased, ate meals, visited in homes, listened, walked, and spent time with each other. They learned how to live life together. In the process, Jesus discipled them. Did they talk Scripture? Did he explain the gospel? Did he apply the Word? Did he set an example for how to live as he lived? Did they wrestle with biblical interpretation? Did they look at their personal problems in light of Scripture? Yes! He did all of that while building relationships with those who followed him. They were not encumbered by a church calendar that kept them so busy in activities they did not have time to be with him and with one another.

Here's what I mean. In one church I served, when I arrived they had a full slate of activities. Things were going on virtually every day. But the church was incredibly unhealthy. They had programs and things to do for every age, but few among them knew how to walk with Jesus. Even most of their classes that were supposed to be Bible studies lacked any real explanation or application of the gospel. Busy? Yes, quite busy. Spiritual? Hardly. Just because a so-called Bible study existed didn't mean disciple-making took place. Maybe that's easier to see when we consider what a disciple is.

What Is a Disciple?

Luke's description of the Jewish council's observation of the disciples, "that they had been with Jesus" (Acts 4:13), aptly explains what being a disciple means. A disciple knows Jesus, spends time with him, grows in relationship to him, follows him, desires to be like him, obeys him, and worships him. Others see the effects of having been with Jesus and it testifies to the power of the gospel. Disciples follow Jesus.

Obviously, through the centuries, some claim to follow Jesus who are not really his disciples. When I pastored in South Alabama in the early 1980s, a couple of robed, bearded, barefooted men came to my office door. The church sat in a curve on a two-lane highway between two communities. These men had walked along the road and found their way to my door. What struck me as I talked with them was what they claimed. "We're followers of Jesus," they said. I immediately asked, "Who is he?" Without batting an eye, one said, "Oh, his name is Lightning Amen, and he lives in Florida." Their reply made it easy to see that professing to follow Jesus doesn't always equate to being a disciple. But others merely professing to be followers of Jesus may not be quite as obvious.

We only follow Jesus *if* we've been regenerated by the Holy Spirit. Jesus told Nicodemus, "You must be born again" (John 3:7). The Pharisee rightly understood that he could not birth himself. God, in grace, had to raise one spiritually dead to life, one enslaved to Satan into freedom, and one living under God's wrath into "the heavenly places in Christ Jesus" (Ephesians 2:6). The Spirit uses the proclamation of the gospel and regenerates us, and we respond with repentance toward God and faith in the Lord Jesus Christ. This gracious work of the triune God brings us into a life of following Jesus as Lord. But what marks this kind of Jesus-following disciple?

1. Disciples trust and follow Jesus as he is revealed in the gospel. They don't devise their own version of Jesus or their own way of salvation. They put their eternal hope in the Jesus proclaimed in Scripture.

2. Disciples are serious about obedience to Jesus. Jesus asked, "Why do you call me 'Lord, Lord,' and not do what I tell you?" (Luke 6:46). He goes on to speak of the one who hears and does what Jesus commands as a person whose house is built upon the rock, which the floods and winds cannot collapse. Obedience does not earn salvation; it just gives evidence that we're following Jesus. We no longer live for ourselves but for Jesus who died and rose again for us (2 Corinthians 5:15).

3. Disciples are serious about understanding and applying God's Word. Speaking to some Jews who professed to believe in Jesus, he told them, "If you abide in my word, you are truly my disciples, and you will know the truth, and the truth will set you free" (John 8:31–32). Jesus made it clear: empty claims mean nothing. Disciples abide in God's Word. They are "doers of the word" (James 1:22) who regularly get reshaped and honed through time in the Word. They long for the Word so that they might grow in Christ (1 Peter 2:2–3).

4. Disciples are serious about serving Jesus by serving others. We sometimes feel the deep burden to serve the Lord. Yet how do we do that? We give cups of cold water in Jesus's name. We visit the sick and imprisoned, welcome the stranger, and clothe the naked, as Jesus said in Matthew 25:31–46. We "love one another" (John 13:34). We "bear one another's burdens" (Galatians 6:2). We "encourage one another" (1 Thessalonians 5:11). We practice "forgiving each other" (Ephesians 4:32). We "accept one another" (Romans 15:7 NASB). The *one another* passages in the New Testament illustrate the seriousness of following Jesus. We don't live for ourselves. Rather, we give ourselves for others in Jesus's name. We manifest obedience to the first great commandment to love God as we obey the second great commandment to love our neighbor. This fact might also help us to see that real discipleship takes place in the community of a local church, as we learn through the ups and downs of life how to live as Christians with one another.

5. Disciples are serious about living the Christian life with others. This reality follows on the heels of serving one another. But more specifically, it implies we don't try to live in a vacuum as Christians or attempt the Christian life alone. We find the model in the book of Acts, as churches were planted and Christians began to live out the gospel together. We also see this model throughout the epistles. Consider how Paul, Peter, and James dealt with relationships in the body. Spend time reading the Pastoral Epistles, noting how they emphasize relationships in the church.

What Is Disciple Making?

The simplest definition of disciple making, as Mark Dever notes, is "helping others follow Jesus." He further explains that disciple making happens by "deliberately doing spiritual good to someone so that he or she will be more like Christ."[3] How can we engage, then, in helping others follow Jesus? When I was a young Christian in the early 1970s, discipleship groups seemed to be the method of choice in making disciples. I'm thankful for time in a few groups where we prayed, read, and discussed God's Word. We applied God's Word to our lives, we fellowshipped, and we held one another accountable as followers of Jesus. I grew in the Lord. Yet there was also the tendency to limit disciple making to the hour or two we spent together. The balance of life didn't figure into the disciple-making equation.

Think about how Jesus trained the Twelve and the seventy-two (sent out in Luke 9 and 10). They spent time with him, received his instruction, and then he sent them in pairs. He modeled life for them. He taught them, most often asking questions to stimulate their thinking about Scripture. He corrected attitudes of superiority, complacency, prejudice, and poor theology. Then he sent them out to put into practice what they had received from and seen modeled by him. They represented him in the towns and villages as they served together in Jesus's name. When the seventy-two returned and reported on their experiences, Jesus "rejoiced in the Holy Spirit" (Luke 10:21). His people lived as *his* followers and served together, causing Jesus to express profound joy. They had discovered a beautiful truth: "The discipling life is an others-centered life."[4] This other-centeredness continues the same pattern of disciple making that has shaped the disciple.

I love the way Jamie Dunlop captures the organic nature of disciple-making: "Discipling should be a mind-set of spiritual intentionality that flows into all manner of friendships—not a program you 'sign up for' and then do in a particular way."[5] Instead of rushing to the latest discipleship program as the new fad among churches, disciple making calls for us to be spiritual people who build relationships centered in Jesus Christ to help people come to know Christ and to mature in him. It's organic rather than programmatic. When the church realizes that to be Christian is to be a disciple, then disciple-making becomes the natural overflow of relationships. That may go against the traditional approach to putting discipleship into a timeslot or particular group or program. Certainly, those things might be useful in making disciples. But it's that "spiritual intentionality that flows into all manner of friendships," as Dunlop reminds us, that best reorients the way a congregation thinks about discipleship. The discipling culture changes when that happens.

How Do You Build a Culture of Discipleship?

My hesitation with any "how do you" heading is that we'll think building a culture of discipleship follows a formula. If we just plug in the right steps, then we'll have a disciple-making congregation. Although it doesn't happen that way, it does seem that God is pleased to change the culture of a congregation through the ordinary means of grace he has entrusted to us. With that in mind, let me identify a few of those means and apply them toward the aim of building a culture of discipleship.

1. Concentrate on preaching expositional sermons through books of the Bible. In doing so, you accomplish a number of features inherent in disciple-making. You take people through the Bible, exposing disciples to the richness of God's Word in all sixty-six books. As you preach Christ from all those parts of the Bible, you will also be teaching Christocentric hermeneutics so that disciples develop the capacity to interpret God's Word in their daily Bible reading—plus those who are not yet disciples will hear the gospel with clarity. Faithful preaching also develops faithful listening, so that disciples' ears get trained to notice details in the Word that affect interpretation and application. And as you preach expositionally, you will regularly be covering issues related to sanctification. You will make disciples as you preach.

2. Pray for disciples to be made and for disciples to mature. Disciple-making is spiritual work. We engage in it, but only the Lord can bring it to fruition. So we pray. Regularly pray through the membership roll of your church. Our church used a prayer card with each family name listed, divided up by days of the week, so that we might pray for one another. Much of my praying for our members has to do with their growth in grace as disciples. Don't forget also to pray for the unbelievers in your sphere of influence. Only the Spirit can bring them to life.

3. Set an example of what it looks like to be a disciple of Jesus. The congregation rightly watches the way their pastors live as Christians. Do you spend time with the Lord daily? Do you lead your family spiritually? Do you treat others with kindness, patience, and humility? Do you honestly love the members of your congregation? You get the idea. If we're not living as disciples, then whatever we plug in programmatically for the church to be disciples will fizzle.

4. Intentionally train potential elders, teachers, pastors, missionaries, and leaders. Rich has referred to the pastoral mentoring we've had at the church I pastored for thirty-five years. We decided that we needed to be intentional in pouring into the spiritual lives of those who might be spiritual leaders in our church or be sent out to other churches. Our pastoral mentoring has been a conduit for elders, pastors, teachers, and missionaries. Here are a few things that you might include in this training:

- Major on "with-ness" (as Günter Krallmann put it). Keep it relational. Be friends in Christ.
- Study Scripture together with a view to faithful interpretation.
- Develop homiletical or teaching structures together through studying the Word.
- Emphasize the application of Scripture to personal and family life.
- Read and discuss good books about doctrine, ecclesiology, polity, preaching, missions, and more.
- Give assignments and opportunities for ministry, with appropriate encouragement and critiques for improvement.

During one season of ministry, I realized the doctrinal poverty among the men in the church. I took them through R. C. Sproul's *Essential Truths of the Christian Faith*, using two or three chapters at each meeting, where I simply asked doctrinally-focused questions as a teaching method. I put the questions together in a workbook so that the men might work on them during the week. It became a pivotal time of revitalization for our church.

5. Offer encouragement to the congregation as you patiently lead them as disciples of Jesus. I include this as a means entrusted to you for building a culture of discipleship. It won't happen by chastising them from the pulpit because of what they're not doing. That produces bitterness, resentment, or legalism. Encouragement certainly has an aspect of admonition, yet it's always to be done with gentleness. "The Lord's servant must not be quarrelsome but kind to everyone, able to teach, patiently enduring evil, correcting his opponents with gentleness. God may perhaps grant them repentance leading to a knowledge of the truth" (2 Timothy 2:24–25).

Trust the Lord to use the means he has given you as you build a culture of discipleship. Expect it to be slow, patient work. Announcing a discipling program doesn't change the culture. The ordinary means of grace blessed by the Spirit do. Only when that happens does disciple making become the natural practice of normal church members. We can be confident that Jesus still rejoices in the Holy Spirit at such a sight.

 Young Pastor Rich Applies the Counsel

No church is perfect. That's not just a worn-out phrase, it's true. One of the dangers as a leader is thinking, *I need to get*

us from point A to point B. And once I lead us to point B, then we will have arrived. Pride underlies that thought. We'll never arrive until we're in Christ's presence. And yet, that's no reason for passivity when it comes to pursuing a culture of discipleship. We're continuing together until Christ is formed in us corporately.

As we began to work toward building a culture of discipleship, our elders tried to model hospitality. We aimed at welcoming people into our lives and homes, growing together in grace, getting to know each other, and praying for and encouraging one another. It was the "with-ness" principle at work. What I noticed is how often I would hear of members fellowshipping together in each other's homes without any coordination from the elders. The body of Christ put into practice what we aimed to model as leaders. By God's grace, the fellowship at Audubon Park grew deeper and richer.

But there's something else I noticed. Church life ebbs and flows. Life has seasons. Showing hospitality, as one example, can't fall on just a few members of the church. It must *continue* being modeled and practiced. That is how culture is created. It becomes the norm.

In God's infinite wisdom, he has designed the church to be a disciple-making people. Discipleship can't be manufactured because a discipling culture is formed out of the fellowship we have in the gospel. We must continue making the Word of God central to the life of the church, modeling what it looks like to follow Jesus. We must keep praying for God to change the culture and training other leaders. We must continue to be and depend on the ordinary means of grace. Finally, we must never underestimate how much we will accomplish over the long haul as we as a church simply enjoy being disciples together.

Mentor Phil Lists Some Next Steps

- Evaluate your ministry in terms of what cultivates disciple-making and what does not. Are there some areas (trellises, as we've mentioned throughout this book) that need to be removed? We suggest doing so with wisdom and patience. Are there some initiatives that need to happen to facilitate disciple-making? Consider what means God has given you to further these initiatives.

- Concentrate on helping the congregation grow in how to read, interpret, and apply Scripture through your weekly exposition. Do you explain how you arrive at a Christ-centered interpretation? Do you make gospel applications, as opposed to applications that lead to legalistic practices? Do you convey joy in the way you handle God's Word?

- Cultivate an organic-relational approach to spreading the gospel in your community. As your members live like Christians, do they naturally talk to others about Christ?

- Encourage the congregation, through layering, to yearly read through God's Word. Provide Bible-reading guides. Use examples in sermons, conversations, and pastoral visits from your own daily Bible reading.

- Consider developing a pastoral internship or mentorship where you engage in training up future leaders. As these trainees grow in grace, they will spread a disciple-making atmosphere throughout the church.

- Set an example as a disciple of Jesus. Years of watching a faithful pastor who lives what he preaches and teaches bears fruit in building a culture of disciple-making.

Recommended Reading

In his book *The Mentoring Church*, Phil explores the way mentoring (another term for disciple-making) best happens in the local church context. He includes historical and contemporary examples for mentoring, as well as a mentoring template adaptable for any sized church. You might also read the following:

Discipling: How to Help Others Follow Jesus by Mark Dever in the 9Marks Building Healthy Churches series

The 9Marks book *The Compelling Community: Where God's Power Makes a Church Attractive* by Mark Dever and Jamie Dunlop

The *9Marks Journal* article, "The Ordinary Means of Grace—Or, Don't Do Weird Stuff," published online in July of 2021 at www.9marks.org

Afterword

Writing this book together has given us a deeper sense of gratitude for all that goes into pastoral ministry. By the Lord's design, we need each other to model, encourage, instruct, correct, and bear burdens in the patient process of pastoral work. Our goal has been to offer a glimpse at how we've put this into practice in our ministries. We hope you find our model, even with its inadequacies, a means to encourage you to persevere and progress in your pastoral ministry.

This book has taken shape through the sharpening work of Jonathan Leeman and Alex Duke of 9Marks Ministries, and Rush Witt, Barbara Miller Juliani, Jack Klumpenhower, and Ruth Castle of New Growth Press. Thank you for partnering with us to serve the broader pastoral community. You've been a joy to work with on this project.

We're especially grateful for Drew Harris, who was part of the pastoral internship cohort with Rich and one of Phil's fellow elders at South Woods, who put his keen eye on helping to edit the work and make suggestions to strengthen it. Thanks, Drew! You've not just lived this book with us, but you've lived in both our pastoral ministries.

(From Phil) Karen, you've listened to me sounding out ideas, welcomed conversations on pastoral ministry, talked me through on phrases, worked on editing and fine-tuning, and prayed for me as I wrote. More than anything, you've shared every detail in my pastoral ministry with grace and encouragement. You're a gift beyond compare!

(From Rich) Kristy, you are God's precious gift to me. My pastoral journey is our journey. You've encouraged me at every step to look to Jesus for joy and help. As I've written, you've prayed for me, encouraged me, shared excellent suggestions, and reminded me so often of God's grace as I've recounted the various seasons of ministry. *An excellent wife who can find?* Found!

(Phil) Mama Jane, I hope this little book dedicated to you will encourage you always to look to Jesus Christ, the Good Shepherd who leads us until we see him face to face.

(Rich) Mom, you and Dad have never wavered in your support and your prayers have never ceased. Keep serving the kingdom of God, for one day we will see what Dad now sees by sight.

(Phil) I'm grateful for thirty-five years of partnership with the saints at South Woods as you've helped me grow as a pastor, regularly encouraged Karen and me, prayed for us and the other pastors and their wives, and listened to the Word with a heart of gladness.

(Rich) Dallas and Don, thank you, brothers, for faithfully co-laboring with me. What a privilege we have to serve Audubon Park together! Audubon Park, we love you and "give thanks to God always for all of you" (1 Thessalonians 1:2).

We know we've only scratched the surface of pastoral ministry and the mentoring we encourage our readers to be part of. But we pray that you've found something of the passion we feel for the incomparable privilege of shepherding the blood-bought church of Jesus Christ.

Notes

Introduction

1. Huldrych Zwingli, *Huldrych Zwingli: Documents of Modern History*, ed. G. R. Potter (London: Edward Arnold, 1978), 65–66, 77. For Zwingli as a mentor, see Phil A. Newton, *The Mentoring Church: How Pastors and Congregations Cultivate Leaders* (Grand Rapids: Kregel, 2017), 83–87.

2. Lifeway Research, *Pastor Attrition Study 2021*, https://lifewayresearch.com/wp-content/uploads/2022/01/Pastor-Attrition-Research-Report-2021.pdf, 28.

3. See the following for additional perspectives on mentoring with these and other historical and present-day pastors: Newton, *The Mentoring Church*, 87–92; Scott M. Manetsch, *Calvin's Company of Pastors: Pastoral Care and the Emerging Reformed Church, 1536–1609* (New York: Oxford University Press, 2013); Michael Haykin, "Robert Hall, Sr. (1728–1791)" in *The British Particular Baptists 1638–1910* vol. 5 (Springfield, MO: Particular Baptist Press, 2000); John Ryland Jr., *The Life and Death of Rev. Andrew Fuller, Late Pastor of the Baptist Church at Kettering, and Secretary to the Baptist Missionary Society, from its Commencement, in 1792* (London: Button and Son, 1818); Timothy George, *Faithful Witness: The Life and Mission of William Carey* (Birmingham, AL: New Hope, 1991); Nathan Finn, "Robert Hall's Contributions to Evangelical Renewal in the Northamptonshire Baptist Association," *Midwestern Journal of Theology* 6.1 (Fall 2007); Derek J. Prime and Alistair Begg, *On Being a Pastor: Understanding our Calling and Work* (Chicago: Moody, 2004); H. B. Charles Jr., *On Pastoring: A Short Guide to Living, Leading, and Ministering as a Pastor* (Chicago: Moody, 2016).

Chapter 1: Get Ongoing Training

1. See the observations on the pastor's walk throughout C. John Miller, *The Heart of a Servant Leader: Letters from Jack Miller*, ed. Barbara Miller Juliani (Phillipsburg, NJ: P&R, 2004).

2. See Timothy S. Laniak, *Shepherds after My Own Heart: Pastoral Traditions and Leadership in the Bible* (Downers Grove, IL: InterVarsity, 2006), 171–222, 235–45.

3. See David Helm, *Expositional Preaching: How We Speak God's Word Today* (Wheaton, IL: Crossway, 2014); D. Martyn Lloyd-Jones, *Preaching and Preachers*, 40th anniversary edition (Grand Rapids: Zondervan, 2011).

Chapter 2: Trust God's Sovereignty

1. Andy Davis, "The Reform of First Baptist Church of Durham," 9Marks website, October 27, 2011, https://www.9marks.org/article/journalreform-first-baptist-church-durham/.

Chapter 3: Now What? Preach the Word

1. J. I. Packer, *God Has Spoken* (Grand Rapids: Baker, 1979), 28.

2. Mark Dever, *Nine Marks of a Healthy Church* (Wheaton, IL: Crossway, 2004), 40.

3. Charles H. Spurgeon, "Christ and His Co-Workers" (sermon, Metropolitan Tabernacle, London, June 10, 1886), spurgeon.org/resource-library/sermons/christ-and-his-co-workers/#flipbook/.

Chapter 4: Aim for Longevity and Biblical Reform

1. Colin Marshall and Tony Payne, *The Trellis and the Vine: The Ministry Mindset that Changes Everything*, 2nd ed. (Kingsford, Australia: Matthias Media, 2021), 8.

2. Marshall and Payne, 8–9.

3. For more detail on the biblical development of the theme of shepherding, see Newton, *40 Questions about Pastoral Ministry*, 17–23 and Laniak, *Shepherds after My Own Heart*.

4. The advice in this section is adapted from Newton, *40 Questions about Pastoral Ministry*, 258–61. Also read and profit from Marshall and Payne's *The Trellis and the Vine*.

Chapter 5: Trust the Word to Minimize or Convert

1. See Matt Merker's helpful 9Marks book *Corporate Worship: How the Church Gathers as God's People* (Wheaton, IL: Crossway, 2021).

Chapter 7: In Desperate Moments, Live in the Gospel

1. Walter Bauer et al., ed., *A Greek-English Lexicon of the New Testament and Other Early Christian Literature*, 3rd ed. (Chicago: University of Chicago Press, 2000), s.v. *pantelés*, 754.

2. Theodore Monod, *Looking unto Jesus*, trans. Helen Willis (Hong Kong: Bible Lite Publishers, n.d., orig. publ. 1862), 18.

Chapter 9: Lead the Church to Biblical Polity

1. Mark Dever and Paul Alexander, *The Deliberate Church: Building Your Ministry on the Gospel* (Wheaton, IL: Crossway, 2005), 33–41. Also see chapter 1 of Dever and Alexander's revised work, *How to Build a Healthy Church: A Practical Guide for Deliberate Leadership* (Wheaton, IL: Crossway, 2021).

2. Mark Dever, *A Display of God's Glory: Basics of Church Structure* (Washington: Center for Church Reform, 2001). Joseph H. Hellerman, *When the Church Was a Family: Recapturing Jesus' Vision for Authentic Christian Community* (Nashville: B&H, 2009).

3. See Matt Schmucker's wonderful discussion of how Capitol Hill Baptist Church in Washington, DC, utilized broadening circles for layering teaching on elders, in Newton and Schmucker, *Elders in the Life of the Church: Rediscovering the Biblical Model for Church Leadership* (Grand Rapids: Kregel, 2014), 59–63.

Chapter 10: Build a Culture of Discipleship

1. Mark Dever, *Discipling: How to Help Others Follow Jesus* (Wheaton, IL: Crossway, 2016), 15.

2. Günter Krallmann, *Mentoring for Mission: A Handbook on Leadership Principles Exemplified by Jesus Christ* (Waynesboro, GA: Gabriel Publishing, 2002), 13–14.

3. Dever, *Discipling*, 13.

4. Dever, 28.

5. Mark Dever and Jamie Dunlop, *The Compelling Community: Where God's Power Makes a Church Attractive* (Wheaton, IL: Crossway, 2015), 121.

9Marks

Building Healthy Churches

9Marks exists to equip church leaders with a biblical vision and practical resources for displaying God's glory to the nations through healthy churches.

To that end, we want to see churches characterized by these nine marks of health:

1. Expositional Preaching
2. Gospel Doctrine
3. A Biblical Understanding of Conversion and Evangelism
4. Biblical Church Membership
5. Biblical Church Discipline
6. A Biblical Concern for Discipleship and Growth
7. Biblical Church Leadership
8. A Biblical Understanding of the Practice of Prayer
9. A Biblical Understanding and Practice of Missions

Find all our titles and other resources at 9Marks.org.